1952-1971

Atlas of Religious Change in America

Peter L. Halvorson
William M. Newman

Cartography by
Mark C. Nielsen

GLENMARY RESEARCH CENTER/WASHINGTON, D.C.

GRC A-62/P-342
October, 1978

The Glenmary Research Center was established in 1966 to help serve the
research needs of the Catholic Church in rural America.

International Standard Book Number: 0-914422-09-X
Library of Congress Catalog Card Number: 78-67653

Contents

Preface/v
Introduction/1

Preface

This *Atlas* is one of several publications resulting from a three year research effort, the various phases of which have been funded by The National Science Foundation, The University of Connecticut Research Foundation, The Hartford Seminary Foundation, and the United Church of Christ Board for Homeland Ministries. Our work was graciously supported by Donald Ploch, Jackson Carroll, and Theodore Erickson at their respective agencies. The project has relied upon the facilities of the University of Connecticut Computer Center, and Social Science Data Center, as well as the cooperation of Phil Jones of the Southern Baptist Convention, Professor Lowell Bennion of Humboldt State University, Alvin Chenkin of the American Jewish Committee, and Bernard Quinn of the Glenmary Research Center. Much of the preliminary data processing was supervised by Jennifer Brown. Computer archive and programming work were done by Bruce Clouette and Robert Krajcik. Special thanks are due to Mark C. Nielsen who did the cartographic work and much more, with skill, patience, and dispatch. John Allen, chair of the geography department at the University of Connecticut has provided moral support and practical assistance throughout. Florence Waxman has gracefully pretended that the mountains of work generated by the project were part of her normal duties as department secretary. Finally, to Fran and Judy our apologies for the countless times this work has intruded into the normal rhythms of life. To all of these and many others not named we express our deepest gratitude. Obviously, we alone bear the responsibility for any errors or shortcomings of this book.

Peter L. Halvorson
William M. Newman

Introduction

SCOPE AND PURPOSE OF THE STUDY

Social scientists and religious leaders alike have long recognized the constraints created by the absence of census or census-type data about American religious groups. While surely none of us would forego the First Amendment freedoms that have kept religious questions out of the United States Census, this has made the study of religious trends in the United States a precarious undertaking. In the early 1950's the National Council of Churches sponsored a unique county level census-type study of religious adherence. Nearly twenty years later, a similar study was jointly sponsored by the Glenmary Research Center, the National Council of Churches, and the Lutheran Church — Missouri Synod. This *Atlas* presents time-series data from these two landmark studies and several supplemental data sources. The 35 groups included in this *Atlas* encompass more than 80 per cent of the reported religious adherence in the United States for the years 1952 and 1971 (see Tables 1 and 2). A series of four maps depicting patterns of distribution and change within and between these years is presented for each of the 35 denominations.

A comparison of Tables 1, 2, and 3 reveals several important aspects of these data. First, as indicated in Table 1, the rate of change in number of adherents varies greatly from denomination to denomination and thus, individual rates differ considerably from the aggregate growth rate for all denominations of 46 percent. Second, as seen in Table 2, this aggregate growth rate for religious groups is significantly higher than that for the total United States population, which was 35 percent between 1950 and 1970. Finally, Table 3 indicates that, like numerical change, spatial change, as measured by the number of counties in which denominations are found, varies greatly from one denomination to another. Moreover, when compared to rates of numerical change, rates of spatial change are somewhat lower. Interestingly, some 20 percent of these denominations have experienced numer-

ical expansion but spatial contraction. All of these facts support the validity and utility of providing accurate pictures of both numerical and spatial change on a denominational basis, and in essence provide the logic for the particular measures that have been mapped in this *Atlas*.

The data archive on which the *Atlas* is based holds the potential for various types of descriptive and analytical studies. The purpose of this publication is descriptive. It is intended to be a reference work for the period 1952-1971. The remainder of the *Introduction* explains the data sources from which the maps have been drawn, the methods employed, as well as the types of maps contained in the *Atlas*. Part 2 contains a series of brief descriptions highlighting the basic trends shown by the maps. The third part of the *Atlas* contains four maps for each of the 35 religious groups, as well as composite patterns for the nation, 144 maps in all. Both the texts in Part 2 and the maps in Part 3 present the denominations in alphabetical order.

DATA SOURCES AND METHODOLOGY

The data mapped in this *Atlas* consist of county level religious adherence statistics. Most of the data are derived from the 1952 National Council of Churches study (Whitman and Trimble 1954) and the similar 1971 Glenmary study (Johnson, Picard, and Quinn 1974). To these we have added several groups from a supplemental data set compiled by the Southern Baptist Convention (Irwin 1976), 1971 statistics for American Jews from the *American Jewish Yearbook,* and a privately circulated data set for Mormons in the Western States (Bennion 1976). A substantial number of mergers occurred among the Protestant groups between 1952 and 1971, necessitating modifications in the original data sources. Accordingly, we have aggregated 1952 data to reflect these mergers. In two cases, the United Church of Christ

TABLE 1

Denominations for Which 1952 and 1971 County Data Are Available

DENOMINATION	ADHERENTS		PERCENT CHANGE
	1952	1971	
American Baptist U.S.A.	1 528 846	1 693 423	11
American Lutheran	1 744 142	2 490 537	43
Baptist General Conference	49 881	125 678	152
Brethren in Christ	6 046	11 458	90
Catholic	29 624 787	44 863 492	51
Christian Reformed	155 007	208 965	35
Church of the Brethren	189 277	220 813	17
Church of God (Anderson)	105 580	389 389	269
Church of God (Cleveland)	136 386	269 989	171
Church of the Nazarene	249 033	869 821	249
Cumberland Presbyterian	93 235	104 070	12
Episcopal	2 544 320	3 032 197	19
Evangelical Congregational	28 476	35 742	26
Evangelical Covenant	52 780	82 453	56
Free Methodist	49 052	63 540	30
Friends	95 499	131 771	38
International Foursquare Gospel	66 191	101 522	53
Jewish	5 112 024	6 113 520	20
Lutheran Church in America	2 481 927	3 010 150	21
Lutheran — Missouri Synod	1 856 633	2 772 996	49
Mennonite	66 900	108 108	62
Moravian — North and South	48 618	57 121	18
Mormons (West only)	822 700	2 016 590	145
N.A. Baptist General Conference	35 265	50 583	43
Pentecostal Holiness	41 555	89 140	115
Presbyterian U.S.	745 627	1 147 499	54
Reformed	194 157	370 509	91
Seventh-Day Adventist	252 554	536 082	112
Seventh-Day Baptist	6 435	6 178	−4
Southern Baptist	8 121 069	14 488 635	78
Unitarian Universalist	159 904	194 733	22
UCC/Congregational	2 013 935	2 411 438	20
United Methodist/Evan. N.A.	9 512 669	11 523 749	21
United Presbyterian U.S.A.	2 670 167	3 546 941	33
Wisconsin Evan. Lutheran	316 642	381 920	21
Total	71 178 238	103 627 402	46

and the United Methodist Church, schisms accompanied mergers. These have required adding 1971 data in order to maintain comparability. Alignments of these data aggregations for 1952 and additions for 1971 are both shown in Table 4.

Several problematic characteristics of these data should be noted. First, the 1952 data contain statistics for 1952 through 1954. Second, in that study two measures, membership and adherents, were reported by some groups. The published reports retained only the larger statistic, adherents, and no record of which denominations pertain to which statistic were kept. Thus, in order to secure comparability for 1971 we have used the Glenmary adherence statistics rather than the smaller member statistics. About two-thirds of the former are estimates based on the latter. Additionally, in both studies different groups have compiled their enumeration employing different age criteria. Again no record of these procedures is available. Furthermore, the Jewish figures for both dates are population estimates rather than actual institutional countings. All of these problems are discussed in greater detail in Newman, Halvorson, and Brown (1977). However, despite these problems, these data are the most comprehensive ever assembled. Granting some degree of stability in reporting procedures within groups, these statistics may appropriately be used to create long term change rates, and thus provide

a unique opportunity to describe patterns of change for a wide range of denominations for the roughly twenty year interval.

The religious data for 1952 and 1971 were entered into a computer file archive. A complete description of the computer tape archive from which the data have been mapped is provided in Halvorson and Newman (1978). Transformations of the data were accomplished with the SPSS computer program (Nie 1975) and preliminary computerized mapping was done using the SYMAP computer program. From these maps master plates were compiled by the cartographer.

TABLE 2

Proportion of Total Church Membership and Total Population Represented in the Longitudinal Archive

	1952	1971	PERCENT CHANGE
Total Members	71 178 238	103 627 402	46
N.C.C. *Yearbook* Totals	87 027 507	124 829 551	43
Percent of Yearbook Totals	82	83	
Total U.S. White Population	134 874 138	178 107 190	32
Percent of U.S. White Population	53	58	
Total U.S. Population	150 697 361	203 212 877	35
Percent of U.S. Population	47	51	

TABLE 3

County Statistics For All Denominations*

DENOMINATION	1952	1971	PERCENT OF COUNTIES IN 1971 (N = 3073)	NET CHANGE	
				No.	Percent
American Baptist U.S.A.	1063	1058	34	−5	−0.5
American Lutheran	875	988	32	113	12.9
Baptist General Conference	170	277	9	107	62.9
Brethren in Christ	49	73	2	24	49.0
Catholic	2556	2817	92	261	10.2
Christian Reformed	122	181	6	59	48.4
Church of the Brethren	458	427	14	−31	−6.8
Church of God (Anderson)	988	993	32	5	0.5
Church of God (Cleveland)	1069	1482	48	413	38.6
Church of the Nazarene	1607	1733	56	126	7.8
Cumberland Presbyterian	303	288	9	−15	−5.0
Episcopal	1942	2033	66	91	4.7
Evangelical Congregational	31	30	1	−1	−3.2
Evangelical Covenant	246	262	9	16	6.5
Free Methodist	575	549	18	−26	−4.5
Friends	242	460	15	218	90.1
International Foursquare Gospel	288	350	11	62	21.5
Jewish	481	504	16	23	4.8
Lutheran Church in America	1039	1146	37	107	10.3
Lutheran — Missouri Synod	1421	1649	54	228	20.3
Mennonite	230	358	12	128	55.7
Moravian — North and South	50	53	2	3	6.0
N.A. Baptist General Conference	145	152	5	7	4.8
Pentecostal Holiness	958	1035	34	77	8.0
Presbyterian U.S.	368	489	16	121	32.9
Reformed	151	203	7	52	34.4
Southern Baptist	1784	2212	72	428	24.0
Seventh-Day Adventist	1462	1624	53	162	11.1
Seventh-Day Baptist	46	45	1	−1	−2.2
Unitarian Universalist	366	520	17	154	42.1
UCC/Congregational	1397	1296	42	−101	−7.2
United Methodist/Evan. N.A.	2881	2955	96	74	2.6
United Presbyterian U.S.A.	1831	1857	60	26	1.4
Wisconsin Evan. Lutheran	248	352	11	104	41.9

*Mormons are excluded due to lack of complete county level data.

MAPPING PROCEDURES

All maps have been created by procedures that permit ease of visual comparison. In each map those counties in which no adherents were reported have been left unshaded. The counties that did have reported adherents for the time period have been arranged in rank order and then trichotomized, creating three categories of equal size. It is important to note that the ranges for the various categories differ markedly from group to group and from map to map within denominations. These ranges must be scrutinized carefully when making comparisons. Each denominational set of four maps appears on two opposing pages, and may be inspected as a set.

The four individual maps for each denomination portray a complete picture of denominational distribution and change for the period from 1952 to 1971. The first map for each denomination depicts the incidence of adherents for the year 1952, while the second shows the same information for 1971. A comparison of these two maps provides the first indication of the stability or change in the relative distribution of a denomination's population between 1952 and 1971. In many cases while the actual magnitude of adherents per county has changed between 1952 and 1971, the relative position of counties in which the group is present, and thus the appearance of the 1952 and 1971 maps, is quite similar.

The third map for each denomination portrays the percent change in adherents during the period under study. These maps may, and, in fact, do show negative numbers. For instance, a county in which a denomination lost its only church and thus no longer has adherents will be shown as a -100 percent loss. Conversely, counties that did not contain adherents in 1952 but in which a new congregation had emerged by 1971 will always produce change rates of exaggerated magnitude. Changes greater than 1000 percent, which includes most counties that groups have newly entered, have been recoded to a value of 1000 percent, thus creating an artificial upper limit for this change measure. In a few instances, usually involving smaller groups, such newly entered counties constitute more than one-third of the total number of 1971 counties. In such instances, the upper category has been enlarged to include all such cases rather than arbitrarily separating cases of equal value. Typically, the change map for each denomination will emphasize "new territory." Important patterns may be discerned by comparing locations of high change rates with previously established patterns of denominational strength (1952) or resulting patterns of strength (1971).

The fourth map for each denomination depicts a measure that is here called shift-share. This is essentially a ratio that shows the extent to which a denomination has changed its share of the total religious adherence in a county between 1952-1971. This ratio has

TABLE 4

**Denominations Requiring Aggregation and/or Addition
Because of Mergers and Schisms Between 1952 and 1971**

DENOMINATION	Adherents	
	1971	1952
American Lutheran	2 490 537	
American Lutheran		800 055
Evangelical Lutheran		895 135
United Evangelical Lutheran		48 952
Lutheran Church in America	3 010 150	
American Evangelical Lutheran		20 234
Augustana Evangelical Lutheran		433 106
Finnish Evangelical Lutheran		29 761
United Lutheran Church in America		1 998 826
Lutheran Church — Missouri Synod	2 772 996	
Lutheran Church — Missouri Synod		1 835 605
Slovak Evangelical Lutheran		21 028
Mennonite Church	108 108	
Mennonite Church		61 903
Conservative Mennonite Conference		4 997
Unitarian Universalist Association	197 733	
Unitarian Church		84 749
Universalist Church of America		75 155
United Church of Christ	2 305 229	
Congregational Christian Churches	106 209	
Congregational Christian Churches		1 263 472
Evangelical and Reformed		750 463
United Methodist	11 511 709	
Methodist		8 790 025
Evangelical United Brethren		722 966
Evangelical Church of N.A.	12 040	
Holiness Methodist		678
United Presbyterian U.S.A.	3 546 941	
Presbyterian U.S.A.		745 627
United Presbyterian of N.A.		221 918
Friends World Committee/America	131 771	
Rel. Soc. Friends, Conservative		1 993
Rel. Soc. Friends, Gen. Conference		16 650
Five Year Meeting of Friends		67 884
Rel. Soc. Friends, Philadelphia		3 748
Central Yearly Meeting of Friends		584
Oregon Yearly Meeting of Friends		4 680

NOTE: The Evangelical Church of North America was formed from a merger of the Holiness Methodist Church and members of the Evangelical United Brethren not participating in the EUB-Methodist Church merger. Since there is no way of counting the latter separately in the 1952 data set, we combined these denominations as United Methodist for both sets.

   Certain Congregationalists did not participate in the United Church of Christ merger. Thus, we added the 1971 Congregational Christian Churches with the United Church.

   The Moravian Church is disaggregated in the 1971 set into North and South groups. We combined the 1971 data into one denomination.

an absolute minimum value of zero. Instances in which a denomination has failed to maintain its share of total religious adherence will register between 1 and zero. Numbers above 1 indicate relative increases. Cases where the shift-share index was greater

than 10.00 have been recoded to a value of 10.00, thereby creating an artificial upper limit for this change measure. As with the percent change map, the upper category in some cases is enlarged by the convention of keeping all equal values in one category. The shift-share ratio may be compared to the previous three maps in several different ways. For instance, it may be found that a denomination has a very high change rate (map 3) in certain counties but that the shift-share ratio (map 4) is close to 1.0. This would indicate that the denomination was simply following a trend of general increase by other denominations in such counties. While the denomination surely grew, its share of religious adherence in that county did not really change. The shift-share ratio may also be compared to geographic areas of established (1952) and emerging (1971) denominational strength.

BIBLIOGRAPHY

American Jewish Committee
   American Jewish Yearbook, annual editions. New York: American Jewish Committee.

Bennion, Lowell
  1976 Privately circulated manuscript containing adherents data for Church of Jesus Christ of Latter-Day Saints for 1971.

Halvorson, Peter L. and William M. Newman
  1978 "A data archive of American religious denominations 1952-1971," *Review of Religious Research,* 20:1 (Fall), 86-91.

Irwin, Leonard G.
  1976 *Churches and Church Membership in the United States Supplementary Data, 1971.* Atlanta, Georgia: Southern Baptist Convention.

Johnson, Douglas, Paul Picard and Bernard Quinn
  1974 *Churches and Church Membership in the United States, 1971.* Washington, D. C.: Glenmary Research Center.

Newman, William M., Peter L. Halvorson and Jennifer Brown
  1977 "Problems and potential uses of the 1952 and 1971 National Council of Churches' 'Churches and church membership in the United States' Studies," *Review of Religious Research,* 18:2 (Winter), 167-173.

Whitman, Lauris B. and Glenn W. Trimble
  1954 *Churches and Church Membership in the United States, 1951.* New York: National Council of Churches.

Analysis of the Maps

American Baptist Churches in the U.S.A.

This denomination was initiated in the North-South split among Baptists that occurred prior to the Civil War. It adopted the name Northern Baptist Convention in 1907, American Baptist Convention in 1950, and American Baptist Churches in the U.S.A. in 1973. It has a congregational polity system and is more liberal on both theological and social issues than its southern counterpart. The ABC numbered 1,528,846 adherents in 1952, and increased 11 percent to 1,693,423 by 1971. In 1971 it reported churches in 1058 counties, 34 percent of all counties.

The ABC countinues to show the effects of its origins. In 1952 only a small cluster of counties in Oklahoma diverge from the north of the Mason-Dixon line distribution. While the group displayed a scattered pattern west of the Mississippi, the primary concentrations were in the northeastern quarter of the country, especially in rural areas such as upstate new York, western Pennsylvania, and southern Indiana. This is true in the sense that there is a continuous distribution and because more counties with sizeable numbers of adherents are found in that portion of the country. By 1971 this distribution had changed in only a limited way. An obvious scattering of isolated counties appear in the southern tier of states. Virtually all are small, probably representing new individual congregations in urban areas. Otherwise, little significant expansion seems to have occurred, and some shrinkage is apparent in the northern Plains states.

The maps of change show a rather mixed pattern. High rates of change, that really represent rates only a bit above the national average, occurred in isolated "new" counties. Most of these are scattered throughout the country, primarily outside of major metropolitan areas. The shift-share map depicts essentially the same pattern, reinforcing the notion that most of the American Baptists' largest growth has been in areas not characterized by rapid overall population growth.

In summary, the ABC does not exhibit significant territorial expansion. Having begun as the "Northern Baptists," it remains essentially a northern denomination that has expanded somewhat into the western states. As will be seen elsewhere, these patterns are in sharp contrast to those of the Southern Baptist Convention.

American Lutheran Church

The American Lutheran Church was formed by a 1960 merger of German (American Lutheran Church), Norwegian (Evangelical Lutheran Church), and Danish (United Evangelical Lutheran Church) branches of American Lutheranism. In 1963 another Norwegian group (Lutheran Free Church) entered the denomination, which has a modified presbyterian form of polity. Adherence increased from 1,744,142 in 1952 to 2,490,537 in 1972, a 43 percent gain. The American Lutheran Church reported churches in 988 counties in 1971, 32 percent of all counties.

The American Lutheran Church traces its beginnings largely to Scandinavian groups, and as might be expected, the 1952 distribution shows an upper midwestern core running from northern Illinois through Wisconsin, Iowa, Minnesota, and into North Dakota. Although the American Lutheran Church is relatively limited in its occurrence, the largest counties do have significant numbers of adherents. Secondary clusters appear in Ohio and Michigan, central Texas, southern California, and the Pacific Northwest. Large areas of the country, however, are almost totally devoid of American Lutheran Church adherents. Included are most of the Rocky Mountain states, the Northeast except for New York City, and the entire southeastern quarter of the nation.

In 1971, the same overall pattern prevails in terms of the location of both the core area and secondary clusters. Close inspection reveals a limited number of new counties scattered in the urban centers of the Southeast (Tennessee, Georgia, and North Carolina) and Rocky Mountain states (New Mexico and Nevada). Additional growth is apparent in southern California and Florida.

The change maps portray somewhat different patterns. The highest category indicates growth rates in excess of ninety percent and appears in some instances within the core area, notably around Minneapolis-St. Paul. Otherwise, the areas of most rapid growth show a distinctly western orientation. They are concentrated on the Plains-Mountain border in Colorado and Montana, and throughout the states bordering the Pacific. Some high growth is in new entry areas in the southeastern and southwestern parts of the country. The shift-share map shows the same pattern, with relatively few areas of strong relative performance in the upper midwest. It is notable that some central cities, such as Minneapolis and Detroit, appear in the lowest category and thus can be seen as areas where the American Lutheran Church has lost considerable ground to other groups. The areas of the greatest relative improvement in strength are in the western states and a few scattered areas in the South.

In summary, the American Lutheran Church is largely a northern group. A continuous distribution extends across the upper Midwest to the Pacific Northwest Coast. Except for a corridor along the Pacific Coast and a cluster in south-central Texas, the rest of the country is largely devoid of counties within which there are American Lutheran Church adherents. This is a regional group that has shown little movement toward becoming a national denomination. Interestingly, a comparison of the 1971 ALC and LCA maps suggests that these two groups have partitioned the northeastern half of the country. The ALC dominates the area west of Ohio, while the LCA is predominant east of the Ohio.

counties appear in a single group. The denomination occupies a total of only 107 counties with the largest single county, Cook County, Illinois (Chicago), containing 9 percent of the national total. By 1971 the distribution had changed in several ways. The number of counties increased by nearly two-thirds. Moreover, the largest single county now is Los Angeles, California, containing 7 percent of the group's adherence. High category adherence counties appear along Puget Sound, at Portland, Oregon, around the Bay Area, and throughout southern California. Although growth is also located in the Midwest, particularly around Great Lakes metropolitan areas, it is not as dramatic there as on the West Coast.

This is the first of several denominations for which the change maps exhibit a slight anomaly. "New" counties make up 38 percent of all 1972 counties. Rather than split the category, all such counties were kept together when the range was trichotomized. This makes the three groups unequal, but avoids an arbitrary division of equal values. Accordingly, on both change maps, all counties in the highest category of both absolute and relative change are new counties and, thus, these two maps appear identical. Moreover, the two lower categories on both maps could indicate fairly sizeable increases. The middle category represents a minimum of 82 percent increases and sizeable gains in the relative share of total religious adherence. While the two local categories are geographically dispersed, relatively few of the lower category are found on the West Coast, suggesting a relative decline for this denomination in the Midwest.

The Baptist General Conference has changed dramatically. It has entered a sizeable number of new counties. Nonetheless, the total number of adherents remains small, and the group is present in 1971 in less than 10 percent of counties, primarily located in only two regions, the West Coast and the upper Midwest. Where once the Baptist General Conference could be characterized as a regional group, it must now be thought of as multiregional.

Baptist General Conference

This denomination was formed by Swedish immigrants during the early 1850's. It adopted the name Swedish Baptist General Conference of America in 1879, and eventually severed its ties with the (then) Northern Baptist Convention in 1944. The term "Swedish" was deleted from its name in 1945. Today, the ethnic characteristic of its membership has greatly diminished. The group practices a conservative version of the Baptist faith. It grew from 49,881 in 1952, to 125,678 adherents in 1971, an increase of 152 percent. In 1971 the Baptist General Conference reported churches in 277 counties, 9 percent of all counties, and a gain of 63 percent since 1952.

The 1952 distribution of this group is entirely consistent with the history of Swedish immigration to the United States. The fringe of Lake Superior and northern Minnesota bound the primary core of adherents. A smaller cluster of contiguous counties surround Chicago, while elsewhere no more than three or four

Brethren in Christ

Most Brethren groups trace their roots to German Baptists, who followed the Pietist reform of established Lutheranism. In America the "River Brethren" or "Brotherhood by the River" resulted from a schism within the United Brethren in Christ in the late 1700's. The River Brethren became the Brethren in Christ in 1863. Their polity is congregational. Increases in adherents from 6,064 in 1952 to 11,458 in 1971 resulted in a 90 percent growth rate. The denomination had churches in 73 counties in 1971, 2 percent of all counties.

The Brethren are yet another small denomination for which these maps can be somewhat misleading. In both 1952 and 1971 the lower limit of the highest category represents 68 and 79 respectively. Thus, in both time periods at least two-thirds of their distribution consists of extremely small numbers of adherents. Moreover, in both time periods, at least 67 percent of the entire denomination was in the State of Pennsylvania, and slightly more than 17 percent of the denomination was in a single county (Lancaster, Pennsylvania).

Predictably, high percent change counties are nearly all counties of new entry for the group. It must be remembered that such counties actually represent very few people. With the exception of several counties in the core Pennsylvania area, high level shift-share counties (in this case both of the upper two categories) mirror the percent change map.

This small group exhibits a slight degree of dispersion, but in reality has only one area of substantial and contiguous density. Most new growth appears to be near counties in which the group was previously established. In both senses, the Brethren in Christ should most accurately be thought of as a highly localized religious sect.

Catholic Church

The Catholic Church is the largest Christian denomination in the United States. It also contains within it a diversity of large ethnic communities. Adherents increased from 29,624,787 in 1952 to 44,863,492 in 1971. This 51 percent gain reflects an increase of over 15 million people. In 1971 the Catholic Church reported churches in 2817 counties, or 92 percent of all counties.

The distribution of Roman Catholic adherents in 1952 and 1971 are essentially the same. In 1952 the areas of greatest strength, which represent almost 3000 members per county, are in the northeastern and southwestern quadrants of the country, with prominent outlying concentrations along the Texas-Louisiana coast, and in the urban areas of the Pacific northwest. By 1971 in addition to these areas of major strength, another somewhat compact area has appeared in Florida. In both periods it is clear that Catholics are found in almost all counties of the nation, but it is also apparent that by 1971 a significant in-filling has occurred in some areas that were noticeably lacking in Catholics in 1952, such as the Deep South and Utah. Thus, the overall pattern of distribution has been rather stable, with one very visible shift toward the Southeast.

That shift is also documented in the other two maps for Roman Catholics. The map depicting percent change projects a reverse image of the first two maps. The areas of greatest change, which in this case is indeed dramatic, are primarily in the Southeast, and in areas of rapid population growth in the western region of the country. Most areas in which there are large numbers of Catholics in both 1952 and 1971, are areas of moderate growth. The areas of slowest growth occur in rural areas of the Great Plains or Rocky Mountain states. The shift-share map provides a somewhat refined view of the same process. The areas in which Roman Catholics most significantly improved their share of total religious adherence are primarily in the southeastern quarter of the country. However, they did not increase their share as markedly in areas like California, which experienced rapid total population growth. In some areas they failed to hold their own. This lowest category is most noticeable in the western half of the nation.

All of these patterns taken together indicate that Roman Catholics are an expanding group. This is true both in terms of their total numbers and in terms of their entrance into new areas such as the South. In that region they have both entered new counties and expanded their share of total adherence in a significant number of counties.

Christian Reformed Church

Reformed Churches trace their beginnings to Calvinism. The Holland Reformed Church withdrew from the Reformed Church in America in the 1830's. By the 1880's it had changed its name to the Christian Reformed Church and absorbed another dissenting group, the True Reformed Church. It has a modified presbyterian polity and practices a conservative version of Reformed Church doctrine. It grew from 155,007 adherents in 1952, to 208,965 in 1971, a 35 percent increase. In 1971 its churches were located in 181 counties, 6 percent of all counties, representing a 48 percent increase since 1952.

This is an ethnic church, still largely comprised of the Dutch of western Michigan. The 1952 map shows four small clusters of adherents: in western Michigan, on the boundary between Iowa and Minnesota, in southern California, and in the Pacific Northwest. However, the category limits indicate that this small group has almost 20 percent of its national total located in Kent County, Michigan. It should also be noted that in 1952 nearly 47 percent of the group was found within the State of Michigan. For this reason, the appearance of wide geographic dispersal of high category adherence counties for this denomination in both 1952 and 1971 is misleading. By 1971, the map seems to indicate considerable transformation. For instance, the number of counties has increased, most noticeably in areas of the West like Colorado, New Mexico, and California. However, virtually all such new counties are in the smallest size category. On the other hand, growth is also apparent in Michigan, which in 1971 still contains 46.1 percent of the total national adherents; and Kent County still holds its unique position.

As is the case for a number of small but growing denominations, the map of percent change can be somewhat misleading. The highest category counties are of course, mostly areas of new entry for the group. However, as noted earlier, these "new" counties also fall within the smallest category in terms of absolute numbers. Moreover, Kent County, Michigan increased by 11,500 adherents, and alone accounts for more than 20 percent of the denomination's national growth. The shift-share map resembles the percent change map and is similarly deceptive. The middle category here includes sizable relative increases, and these counties are located in the small core areas previously identified on the 1952 map.

The Christian Reformed Church has experienced substantial expansion in both adherents and territory. Nonetheless, the actual and symbolic center of the denomination remains in "Little Holland," Michigan. In some sense, the pattern of the Christian

Reformed Church can be viewed as a mini-version of the Mormon pattern in the West.

Church of the Brethren

The Church of the Brethren was formed in the United States in the early 1700's. It consisted of German Pietists fleeing persecution. Pacifism is an important aspect of Brethren theology. They also published the first German bible in America in the mid-1700's. The Seventh-Day Baptists, the New Dunkards (Church of God), Old Order Dunkards, and Progressive Brethren were all formed through schisms within this denomination. They grew from 189,277 in 1952 to 220,813 in 1971, a 17 percent increase. In 1971 they had churches in 427 counties, 15 percent of all counties, representing a slight decrease of 7 percent since 1952.

In 1952 the core area of the denomination begins in southern Pennsylvania, stretches into Maryland and down the Shenandoah Valley in Virginia. These three states account for over 48 percent of the group's national adherents. The lower Midwest and West Coast also contain strong clusters of counties. Like several other small denominations, such as the Wisconsin Lutherans and the Pentecostal Holiness Church, the Brethren experienced increasing proportional strength in the original core area. In 1971, the three-state core contains nearly 52 percent of the national adherents. This pattern was accompanied by numeric increase but geographic shrinkage.

Low values are dominant in the lower two categories of both the percent change and the shift-share map. These indicate both absolute and relative declines for the denomination in more than a third of its counties. Such counties are found more frequently away from the eastern core area, which generally showed stronger performance.

The Church of the Brethren began as a regional group. By 1952 it had already made an incursion into the Midwest. Yet, between 1952 and 1971, in spite of numeric growth, it barely held its position geographically. In this sense the period has meant a re-emphasis of the denomination's regional character.

Church of God (Anderson, Indiana)

Several hundred holiness, sanctification, and revivalist native American churches use the name "Church of God." The Church of God (Anderson, Indiana), derives from a schism in the parent group, General Eldership of the Church of God, which itself began in the 1820's. The Anderson group calls itself an association or movement, not a denomination. While it is a conservative movement, practicing foot washing and immersion, it does not

condone speaking in tongues. It grew from 105,580 adherents in 1952, to 389,989 in 1971, a 269 percent increase. In 1971 it reported churches in 993 counties, 32 percent of all counties.

The Church of God (Anderson) in 1952 displays a curiously diffuse pattern. Although its primary cluster is in a midwestern triangle bounded by West Virginia, central Michigan, and Buffalo, other smaller cores appear on the west coast, and in Oklahoma and Kansas. It should be noted that the lower limit of the largest size class is quite small, representing a minimum of 85 persons per county. Elsewhere, the group is present in randomly scattered counties, isolated counties, and small sets of counties. By 1971 the distribution has undergone negligible changes. The 1952 and 1971 maps are very similar, with the midwestern core areas virtually identical. Change that has occurred is only indicated by differences in the category limits on the two maps. In every instance such comparisons reveal increases of more than threefold. The stability of the pattern on these maps means that most of this denomination's growth occurred within areas of established strength, probably within existing congregations.

The change maps confirm this assertion. The two highest categories of change represent growth rates of at least 149 percent. A significant proportion of such counties are located in the West and South, particularly in Florida. However, their prevalence throughout the midwestern core area reinforces the image of growth within existing centers of strength. The shift-share map is strikingly similar, indicating that absolute and relative change rates are strongly associated. Moreover, the two higher category limits indicate very strong relative performance by this group. Such counties appear in all regions where the Church of God (Anderson) is located, but are most common in the midwestern core area.

This group should be compared with its counterpart, The Church of God (Cleveland, Tennessee). The Church of God (Anderson) appears more northern in its orientation, and has experienced much less regional shift despite having grown rapidly in adherents. The Church of God (Anderson) continues to have a strong regional orientation, and experienced rapid numerical growth from 1952 to 1971. Most of that growth was contained within areas where the denomination had already been established prior to 1952.

Church of God (Cleveland, Tennessee)

The Church of God (Cleveland, Tennessee) was formed in 1886 as the "Christian Union" under the leadership of Richard Spurling. It was renamed "The Holiness Church" in 1902 under A. J. Tomlinson's leadership. This group underwent a number of schisms through the 1920's, with the Church of God (Cleveland) being the largest survivor of these disputes. These are "born again" Christians, practicing speaking in tongues and divine healing. The denomination grew from 136,386 adherents in 1952, to 269,989 in 1971, an increase of 171 percent. In 1971 it had churches in 1482 counties, 48 percent of all counties and representing an increase of 39 percent since 1952.

The distribution of this denomination in 1952 was clearly regional. Although a very random scattering of counties with Church of God (Cleveland) adherents was present west of the Mississippi and in the Northeast, the denomination was clearly concentrated in the Southeast. One concentration ran along the Appalachians from central Alabama to southern Pennsylvania, while another ran along the coast from the Carolinas through the Florida peninsula. By 1971 vigorous expansion is obvious, with considerable numbers of counties added in the far West, the Great Lakes region, and the Northeast. Interestingly, a significant number of these new counties fall in the highest size category.

The maps of change further clarify this picture of rapid expansion. The lowest category of percent change, found most frequently in the southeastern core area, includes positive change rates in excess of 100 percent, indicating growth has been very significant within the old core area. However, the highest rates of change are largely outside of the Southeast and, as they consist primarily of counties of new entry, are concentrated in the areas of the West, Midwest, and Northeast already identified. The shift-share map conveys much the same impression of strong growth. Even the lowest category here contains strong relative growth counties.

The Church of God (Cleveland) has begun a process of transformation much like that of the Southern Baptists. During this period it has moved strongly beyond its original base in the Southeast into most other parts of the nation. In this way the group contrasts strongly with its companion denomination, the Church of God (Anderson), which despite strong numeric growth, has not changed appreciably in its geographic distribution.

Church of the Nazarene

A major revivalist movement, the National Holiness Movement, emerged in America during the Civil War era. Substantial numbers of independent Methodist-type groups formed new denominations. Four such groups merged in 1908 to create the Church of the Nazarene. It is a moderate form of Pentecostalism, does not condone speaking in tongues, and follows Methodist-type polity and discipline. Between 1952 and 1971 they grew from 249,033 to 869,821 adherents, a 249 percent increase. In 1971 they had churches in 1733 counties, 56 percent of all counties.

This denomination grew dramatically between 1952 and 1971. The 1952 pattern is spotty, with "islands" in which the group was present in substantial numbers and in a significant number of counties. The three separate clusters were in the Midwest, from western Pennsylvania to eastern Illinois, the Southern Plains, from north Texas into central Kansas, and along the Pacific Coast. In other areas of the country such as the Mountain States, the Northern Plains, and some parts of the Southeast, large numbers of counties had no reported Nazarene adherents. Notably, the lower size limit for large counties was only 120 adherents. By 1971 this lower limit had risen to more than 360, illustrating the considerable expansion of the group. The same clusters of strength are apparent for 1971, with some expansion visible in the Midwest and on the West Coast. Counties into which Nazarenes had made new entry were in the Northeast and Southeast, with large parts of the Mountain States, Northern Plains, and south Texas still lacking Nazarene adherents.

The change maps show a somewhat different pattern. The two central clusters do not have many counties of the highest category of change (i.e. those representing growth of more than 400 percent). Rather, such high growth counties are located on the fringes of these two clusters, especially in the West. Otherwise, high growth rate counties are in newer areas of expansion such as northern New England, Florida, and South Carolina. The shift-share map is quite similar, and it should be noted that both of the upper categories represent significant relative increases in the number of adherents. The rapid growth areas of Florida and southern California, as is the case for many other denominations, register stronger percent change than relative growth.

By 1971 the Church of the Nazarene is rather widespread and experiencing rapid growth. Although much of this growth appears within or adjacent to areas of established Nazarene strength, there has also been some clear expansion into new areas. Thus, despite being thinly spread in some areas, the group appears to be in the process of becoming more national in its distribution. Continued rapid expansion, as evidenced here, would make this a ranking national denomination.

Cumberland Presbyterian Church

The Cumberland Presbyterian Church was a product of the expanding American West and the Second great Awakenings in the early 1800s. It was an attempt at a less "rigid" form of Presbyterianism (i.e. Calvinism). A merger in 1906 between this group and the Presbyterian Church, U.S.A. (now called United Presbyterian Church, U.S.A.) precipitated a split. This denomination consists of churches not entering the merger. Between 1952 and 1971 they grew from 93,235 to 104,070 adherents, a 12 percent increase. In 1971 churches were reported in 288 counties, 9 percent of all counties, representing a slight (5 percent) decrease since 1952.

The 1952 map of the Cumberland Presbyterian Church depicts a regional group appropriately centered on the Cumberland Plateau. The core area is located in western Tennessee and Kentucky, and extends slightly into the southern Appalachians through Tennessee and northern Alabama. A very limited distribution of scattered counties appears in adjacent states, primarily to the west of the core area. Isolated counties in both California and Detroit serve to further accentuate the extreme regionalism of the group. The 1971 distribution shows a slight decrease in the number of counties containing Cumberland Presbyterians, especially outside the core area, but no change in the basic distribution. The category limits on these two maps reflect the moderate growth of the denomination.

The maps of absolute and relative change have one strong similarity. In both instances, only the uppermost category indicates any appreciable increase. The highest category of percent increase is about evenly divided between the core area and more isolated clusters. The growth has not been regional in the strict sense, but is exclusively within previously established areas. However the area of decline is primarily located in the tier of secondary locations immediately to the west of the core area. The shift-share map is quite similar in terms of the distribution of both the high growth rate counties and the areas of greatest relative decline.

The Cumberland Presbyterians began as a small splinter group and continue to appear as such. They have a regional distribution, with no consistent pattern of growth outside of the areas within which they were already established by 1952. Furthermore, they lost ground both absolutely and relatively in some areas where they were less well established.

Episcopal Church

The Protestant Episcopal Church is the American branch of the Anglican Church or Church of England. It was the only major Protestant group in America not divided by the Civil War. Yet, in the late 1970's a schism emerged that is not reflected in these data, between the Episcopal Church and the new Anglican Church of North America. The issue was the ordination of women. Between 1952 and 1971 the Episcopal Church grew from 2,544,320 to 3,032,197 adherents, a 19 percent increase. In 1971 churches were reported in 2033 counties, 65 percent of all counties.

The Episcopal Church is basically a national church that nonetheless, is absent from a large number of counties. As the 1952 and 1971 maps show, the group is present in all regions but is missing from many counties especially in the more agrarian middle section of the country. That this group is a relatively small segment of total church adherence in most areas is suggested by the fact that 2 or 3 modestly sized churches might contain enough people to place a county in the highest category on both maps. For example, some areas of sparsely populated Wyoming are designated as significant concentrations of Episcopalians. Historically, the Episcopal Church has had strong associations with the colonial Northeast and in 1971 still had much of its strength there. Significant secondary concentrations have developed in the upper Midwest from Detroit to Chicago, and in both southern California and Florida.

The maps depicting change for Episcopalians show a different pattern than the maps of absolute incidence. It is important to note that the lowest category here represents decline, and that this category appears throughout the country, from heavily populated metropolitan areas in the Northeast and Midwest, to more sparsely populated areas in the West. Similarly, the counties of highest growth are scattered randomly throughout the country, although such cases are relatively infrequent in the northeastern core area. The shift-share map shows that in some areas of relatively high growth, particularly in the western states and in Florida, the Episcopal Church has not kept pace with the general rate of population growth. Areas in which Episcopalians have increased their share of membership are scattered throughout the country but are also mostly outside areas of their greatest absolute strength. In the metropolitan counties of the Northeast and Midwest, which appear to be the core of the denomination, the Episcopalians have either lost ground (lowest category) or barely held their own.

In summary, the Episcopal Church is a national denomination, thinly spread across much of the nation. The counties exhibiting the highest growth rate between 1952 and 1971 are outside the denomination's areas of traditional strength. While this growth has been modest, its effect has been to make the Episcopal Church even less regionalized.

Evangelical Congregational Church

In 1922 a reunion between the Evangelical Association and the United Evangelical Church created the Evangelical Church. The Evangelical Congregational Church was formed by churches dissenting in that merger. Their faith is Methodism, but they grant substantial autonomy to local congregations. Between 1952 and 1971 they grew from 28,476 to 35,742 adherents, a 26 percent increase. In 1971, they had churches in 30 counties, less than 1 percent of all counties.

This very small group is almost exclusively located in Pennsylvania. In 1952 they reported only eleven non-Pennsylvanian counties, mostly in Ohio and Illinois, and all are in the smaller size categories. By 1971 this distribution had changed noticeably, but there still were only fifteen counties outside Pennsylvania, and fully 89 percent of the adherents were in Pennsylvania. The strong and persistent cluster of counties in the southeastern portion of that state is particularly notable on both maps.

The change maps show similar patterns of both relative and absolute growth within the core area of Pennsylvania. Outside southeastern Pennsylvania, counties exhibit both advance and retreat. Interestingly, declines tend to be total, while advances are mostly instances of new entry.

This very small group is highly regional, almost totally confined to one corner of a single state. They give no evidence of a major geographic shift. They are likely of secondary cultural importance within their core area, as this portion of Pennsylvania is strongly associated with the Pennsylvania Dutch, meaning the Amish and other Mennonites.

Evangelical Covenant Church of America

This small denomination traces its theology to Continental Lutheranism and its American formation to the revivals of the 19th century. The Covenant Church increased from 52,780 adherents in 1952 to 82,453 adherents in 1971, a rate of 56 percent. In 1971 it reported churches in 262 counties, less than 10 percent of all counties.

As might be anticipated from the preceding description, the 1952 distribution of this group is strongly northern. While the pattern is hardly continuous, a series of small clusters are located in southern New England and Minnesota, as well as the San Francisco, Seattle, and Chicago areas. Across the entire southern tier of states east of California, only five counties contain adherents of this group. The 1971 distribution is basically the same. While a handful of new counties have appeared in the South, the distribution remains both northern and scattered in essentially the same small clusters. Interestingly, Cook County, Illinois (Chicago) contains almost 10 percent of this denomination's adherents in 1971. The remainder of the distribution is relatively thin.

The change maps give a rather different image. Both the Northeast and upper Midwest show high growth rates, but much less than the western population centers. It is also striking that all of the isolated counties in the southeast have experienced high growth rates. The shift-share map provides a similar picture of change in a regional sense, although a number of counties in the Northwest and Southeast had less relative than absolute growth.

Overall the Evangelical Covenant Church is best viewed as a numerically small and spatially fragmented denomination. It does not possess a strongly defined core area, nor does it have a clear regional growth trend between 1952 and 1971. Although its rate of growth over the period was high, it should be remembered that these are relatively small absolute numbers that did not entail territorial expansion.

Free Methodist Church of North America

The Free Methodist Church was founded in 1860. It originally consisted of conservative Methodists objecting to the revivalist or 'new school' ideas and practices that were sweeping the churches during the Second Great Awakening. The Free Methodists insist on strict compliance with Wesleyan doctrine and discipline. Between 1952 and 1971 they grew from 49,052 to 63,540 adherents, a 30 percent increase. In 1971 they reported churches in 549 counties, 18 percent of all counties.

The Free Methodists are a small group and, given the number of counties in which they are located, are rather thinly spread across wide areas of the nation. The 1952 map portrays a scattering of counties from coast to coast, largely in the northern segment of the country. Areas with significant clusters of contiguous counties, containing nearly 100 adherents each, include western Pennsylvania and New York, Michigan, and a series in West Coast metropolitan locations. Between Michigan and the West Coast the pattern is largely discontinuous. From 1952 to 1971 the Free Methodist Church of North America experienced a moderate increase in adherents and a slight decrease in the number of counties in which it is found. The 1971 pattern holds few surprises, with the same core areas appearing along the West Coast, in Michigan, and from Pennsylvania through New York. A few more counties do appear in the Southeast but all represent very few adherents.

The two change maps are different from the 1952 and 1971 adherence maps. The percent change map shows a bias toward the West in terms of highest growth rates on the margins of the region rather than at its center. Elsewhere, the high growth rate counties are scattered randomly throughout the remainder of the Midwest and Plains states, as well as the new entry counties of the Southeast. The shift-share map shows yet a different picture of this growth. On the West Coast and in Florida, despite a high growth rate, the denomination didn't keep pace with the increase in total religious adherence. Moreover, the lowest shift-share category represents counties in which the Free Methodists lost considerable ground to other denominations.

The Free Methodist Church of North America is a small, widely scattered denomination that between 1952 and 1971 augmented its regional midwestern core with similar concentrations in several West Coast communities. In absolute members their growth has been modest, and in various locations they have even experienced shrinkage.

Friends

The Friends, or Quakers, trace their beginnings to the teachings of the Englishman George Fox in the seventeenth century. Fleeing persecution, they found refuge and prosperity in Pennsylvania in the eighteenth century. They are known for their philosophy of pacifism and the work of the American Friends Service Committee. The data used here are supplied by the Friends World Committee and encompass six different branches of American Quakerism. Between 1952 and 1971 they grew from 95,499 to 131,771 adherents, a 38 percent increase. They reported churches in 460 counties in 1971, 15 percent of all counties, representing a 90 percent increase since 1952.

By 1952 the Friends had dispersed from their original Pennsylvania base to a series of other clusters across the nation, most notably in Indiana and Iowa. However, with the exception of three secondary clusters in California, Colorado, and North Carolina, the group showed a strong orientation to the northeastern quarter of the country. By 1971 the number of counties containing Friends adherents had almost doubled. In addition to counties with large numbers of adherents in both 1952 and 1971, significant new areas of strength appeared in the Pacific Northwest, the southern Plains, Florida, and southern New England.

As is the case with a few other small groups, the change maps highlight the counties of new entry. In this instance the new counties comprise 47 percent of the 1971 total and thereby greatly imbalance the three categories in a numerical sense. Nonetheless, the pattern of expansion of the group into new areas is graphically portrayed on both maps. It should be noted that the cut-off between the two lower categories in both instances is moderate. Taken in conjunction with a 38 percent increase in absolute numbers, growth rates in the "old" counties have lost ground relative to growth in total religious adherence.

The Friends present a somewhat complex picture. Overall numerical growth has not been spectacular, and change rates in previously occupied counties have not been very high. Conversely, the group has moved into a large number of new counties in a variety of regions. The group has yet to enter large areas in the South and in the northern Plains but it is clearly no longer a regional sect.

International Church of the Foursquare Gospel

Centered in Los Angeles, this denomination was founded in 1923 by the evangelist Aimee Semple McPherson. Its doctrines are both Adventist and fundamentalistic. This native American form of Protestantism has spread to 27 different countries through missionary work. Between 1952 and 1971 they grew from 66,191 to 101,522 adherents, a 53 percent increase. In 1971 their churches were located in 350 counties, 11 percent of all counties, representing a 22 percent gain since 1952.

The 1952 pattern of the Foursquare Gospel Church reflects the date and location of its founding. California, which in 1952 contained 59 percent of the denomination's adherents, and several adjacent areas on the West Coast and in Arizona constitute the original core area. Otherwise, the group was scattered across the nation, with some secondary clusters in Colorado, Illinois, Ohio, and Texas. By 1971, this pattern had changed. New counties became scattered rather evenly across the nation, and the distinctly California character of the denomination diminished, with only 35 percent of the adherents located in that state by then.

The change maps corroborate the impression of decreasing West Coast dominance. Most West Coast counties fall in the middle percent change category, indicating some positive growth, although a few were "losers." However, most of the highest growth rate counties were located from Colorado eastward, and are not restricted to particular types of counties or regions. The shift-share map is quite similar. The strongest West Coast performances are north of the southern California core area. The largest number of high growth rate counties are east of the Rockies. While increases in relative strength do not follow clear regional lines, a significant number of the lowest category counties, indicating relative decline, are in southern California and elsewhere along the West Coast.

Its twentieth century and West Coast origins make this group rather unique. In 1971 the West Coast orientation still prevails, but between 1952 and 1971 changes were clearly diminishing this dominance. The pattern of change or growth does not possess clear regional direction but rather, is spread across the country.

Jewish Population

Jews are the largest non-Christian religious minority in the United States, about 3 percent of the adult population. They arrived here in the 1650's establishing congregations in New Amsterdam, and Newport, Rhode Island. Important denominational divisions within Judaism, Orthodox, Conservative, and Reform, are not reflected in these data. These are estimates of communities with 100 or more Jewish adherents. Between 1952 and 1971 the Jewish population grew from 5,112,024 to 6,113,520 people, a 20 percent gain. In 1971 Jewish communities of 100 or more people were reported in 504 counties, 16 percent of all counties.

The absolute distribution of the Jewish population as reported in these statistics is one of the most distinctive in the entire *Atlas*. This sizeable group is strikingly concentrated in a limited number of counties in both 1952 and 1971. In both instances, the areas of highest incidence, representing more than 1000 people, are in the "megalopolitan" counties of the northeastern coastal fringe and southern California, with other clusters around the southern Great Lakes. Outside of these areas, although the pattern may appear to be unstructured, it is actually a good surrogate for a map of urban areas in both 1952 and 1971. There are few significant regional shifts on these maps, although close inspection suggests evidence of suburbanization around some of the major population centers.

The maps of change show a somewhat different pattern. The areas showing the highest percentage of increases and the only increases significantly above the national population growth rate, fall into four separate categories. First, are suburban areas in the Northeast, where a number of central city areas show declines. Second, an area of high percentage of growth occurs in the rapidly expanding southern and western metropolitan clusters from Texas to California. The third area of highest growth rate is the Southeast, especially in the smaller urban centers. Finally, there are a series of "sun belt" retirement centers in Florida and Arizona. The map depicting the shift-share for Jews shows these same patterns. For the Jews only the highest category represents any relative increase in adherence. The areas of greatest absolute numbers that also show a growth in the share of total membership are confined to a few major urban areas in the South and West, and the suburban areas of the Northeast. Otherwise, the most marked increase in this index are found in areas of the country that are less stereotypically Jewish, particularly lesser urban centers of the eastern half of the country.

The lowest category, representing declines in Jewish adherence, are similarly distributed throughout the nation. In some instances, these are major central cities, such as New York and Chicago, that are situated next to growing suburban counties. However, it is also clear from a comparison of the percent change and shift-share maps that in smaller cities such as Oklahoma City, Omaha, San Antonio, and several other locations in Texas, declines in Jewish adherence have been relative but not absolute.

In summary, these patterns depict some very major shifts within the distribution of American Jewry both from central city to suburb and from the Northeast to the South and West. Nonetheless, the Jewish population continues to be located within a limited number of counties throughout the country as a whole. This pattern is unique.

Lutheran Church in America

This is the largest branch of American Lutheranism. It was created by a 1962 merger of the United Lutheran Church (itself the result of a 1918 merger), the Augustana Evangelical Lutheran Church (Swedish), the American Evangelical Lutheran Church (Danish), and the Finnish Evangelical Lutheran Church (the Suomi Synod). Between 1952 and 1971 this denomination grew from 2,481,927 to 3,010,150 adherents, a 21 percent increase. In 1971, LCA churches were located in 1146 counties, 37 percent of all counties.

The Lutheran Church in America shows the legacy of its ethnic beginnings as clearly as does its companion group, the American Lutheran Church. The Lutheran Church in America is an amalgam of Scandinavian and German ethnic denominations. Consequently, the areas of strength in 1952 are almost exclusively in the northeastern quarter of the country, specifically in a continuous band from Boston to Cleveland, with considerable secondary strength in southern Wisconsin and northern Illinois. Smaller concentrations occur farther west, from central Kansas to northern Minnesota, and in three quite separate areas, the Pacific Northwest, southern California and the Carolina Piedmont. The 1971 pattern is not very different, the main areas of strength continuing to be in the northeastern quarter of the nation, with secondary clusters as previously described. Moreover, there are relatively few areas of significant new entry. A few new counties appear in the Southeast (particularly in Florida), in the Southwest (west Texas and southern New Mexico), and on the Pacific Coast from San Francisco north to Washington.

The change maps are quite different from those portraying the actual distribution of adherents for the Lutheran Church in America. The counties that experienced the fastest growth rates, all of which are more than twice the national population growth rate, are primarily located in the western part of the country and in the Deep South. A small number of such counties are located in the core area of the Northeast. The shift-share map shows a similar pattern with only minor differences. In a number of rapidly growing western and southern urban areas such as Seattle, Miami, and southern California, the Lutheran Church in America failed to keep pace with growth in total religious adherence. The areas of relative decline are quite continuous throughout the Northeast, and indicate that the group is growing more rapidly in marginal or new regions outside those of its traditional strength.

In summary, the Lutheran Church in America, like its companion group the American Lutheran Church, remains relatively regional in its distribution. Both groups are found predominantly in the northeastern portions of the country and have made relatively limited inroads into other regions, particularly the Rocky Mountain states and the Southeast. Thus while all of American Lutheranism provides substantial coverage nation wide, no single Lutheran denomination, including the Lutheran Church in America, is yet truly national in character.

Lutheran Church — Missouri Synod

Founded in 1847 as the German Evangelical Lutheran Synod of Wisconsin, this has been the most conservative major American Lutheran group. In 1964 it absorbed a Finnish group, the National Evangelical Lutheran Church. In the mid-1970's the Missouri Synod was torn by a theological controversy, resulting in a schism and a new church named the Association of Evangelical Lutheran Churches. Between 1952 and 1971 the Missouri Synod grew from 1,856,633 to 2,772,996 adherents, a 49 percent increase. In 1971, it reported churches in 1659 counties, 54 percent of all counties, representing an increase of 20 percent since 1952.

The Missouri Synod, as its name implies, is of midwestern origin. The 1952 distribution shows a core area extending from eastern Michigan into the Great Plains. The smallest category, which in many instances probably represents a single congregation per county, occurs throughout the western half of the country and in a random scattering in the Southeast. The 1971 map begins to depict some of the substantial growth that has occurred. First, the lower limit for the highest category has increased by almost 50 percent. This means that counties in the midwestern core remaining in this category have experienced very significant expansion. New counties in this highest category also appear in southern California, Arizona, and Florida. Some growth is also apparent in the Boston-Washington corridor. In comparison to other Lutheran groups, by 1971 the Missouri Synod has considerably more national coverage, even though large areas show only a thin distribution.

The map depicting percent change shows a familiar pattern. The areas of highest growth, in this case in excess of 140 percent, are mostly outside of the denomination's area of traditional strength. Substantial growth surrounds the midwestern states, with many such counties in the western half of the country. There are also high growth areas from Texas to Florida in the South, and a smaller cluster in the Northwest. While the Midwest does possess some counties experiencing the highest growth rates, these are widely scattered. This core area contains many counties in the middle change category. Noting the category limits, these could represent quite sizeable growth. The shift-share map follows this pattern to a significant degree. Again, areas showing the most relative growth appear to be mostly outside the Midwest. Although many such counties are found in the western part of the country, high relative increases appear with greater frequency through the South.

The Missouri Synod obviously has been the most rapidly growing of the three major Lutheran groups, in both total adherents and in the number of new counties. In that process it has become the most national of the Lutheran groups. Yet, it is still absent from enough counties, particularly in the South, to prevent its being called a national denomination, even though a regional label is also no longer accurate.

Mennonite Church

The Mennonites are named for Menno Simons, a founder of the Anabaptist or radical right wing of the Reformation. They were persecuted in much of Europe and fled to America in 1683. Numerous conservative Baptist groups have developed in the Anabaptist (literally re-baptizers) tradition, among them, the Mennonite, Hutterite, Amish, and Brethren denominations. Between 1952 and 1971 the Mennonite Church grew from 66,900 to 108,108 adherents, a 62 percent increase. In 1971 they reported churches in 358 counties, 12 percent of all counties and an increase of 56 percent since 1952.

In 1952 the popular sterotype of the Mennonites as located only in the so-called Pennsylvania Dutch country was already inaccurate. Southern Pennsylvania did account for 38 percent of the denomination, with the strongest single concentration in Lancaster County, which reported 19 percent. Yet, the 1952 map indicates sizeable groupings of Mennonites in Ohio, Illinois, and Indiana, and relatively weak isolated counties and small clusters of counties in the western states. The 1971 map indicates strong growth in several areas. Much of this growth occurred in counties close to preexisting clusters, such as in northern Pennsylvania. Additional growth was also in evidence in a wide range of locations scattered across the nation.

These changes are more easily viewed on the two change maps, which are virtually identical. The entire top category of the percent change map, are counties of new entry. The decreasing proportions of adherents located in 1971 in Pennsylvania (34 percent) and Lancaster County (less than 16 percent) fit with the image of high growth counties scattered throughout the nation, and especially outside the southern Pennsylvania core area.

These maps clearly refute the characterization of the Mennonites as a highly localized sect. Like several other smaller groups, they continue to exhibit an original core area. However, the Mennonite Church has become geographically dispersed into all but six states, and has grown especially in nonmetropolitan areas. Numerically it may be accurate to depict them as a minor sect, but their 1971 distribution is clearly a national one.

Moravian Church — North and South

Moravians and Bohemians emerged in opposition to Catholicism well before the Reformation. These Brethren, or *Unitas Fratrum* were widely persecuted and migrated from Germany to America in the 1730's. They are an evangelical group practicing infant baptism. Between 1952 and 1971 their combined North and South provinces grew from 48,618 to 57,121 adherents, an 18 percent increase. They have churches in 53 counties, 2 percent of all counties.

As both the 1952 and 1971 maps indicate, the Moravian Church has two major areas of adherence. The larger of these is in the State of North Carolina. In both periods, the single area of Forsyth County, North Carolina contained over 30 percent of the entire denomination. The second area of concentration grows outward from the Delaware River Valley in the States of Pennsylvania and New Jersey. In 1952 the remainder of the denomination consists of either small clusters or isolated counties in the upper midwestern states. By 1971, there are very few changes in this distribution. A few counties in North Carolina have been lost, an instance of stable numbers but shrinking geographic coverage. The most obvious new incursions are in California and Florida.

The change maps illustrate that geographic dispersion into new areas has been counterbalanced by a pattern of absolute and relative declines in areas where the Moravians had previously been established. This is shown by the category limits. The middle category of the percent change map includes negative figures, and the upper category of the shift-share map includes some areas of relative decline. Thus, in the majority of counties where they were found, the Moravians experienced either absolute or relative declines.

During a period when American religion made impressive absolute gains and advances relative to population change, the North and South divisions of the Moravian Church present a picture of stability. This remains a very small multiregional sect.

Mormons (Latter-Day Saints)

The Church of Jesus Christ of Latter-Day Saints is the largest of five different Mormon groups in the United States. Founded by Joseph Smith in the 1830's, they were banished first from New York State, and later Ohio, Missouri, and Illinois, before settling in Utah. Baptism for the dead and sealing in marriage for eternity are distinctive Mormon practices. National level statistics shows this group increasing between 1952 and 1971 from 822,700 to 2,016,590 adherents, a 145 percent increase. Unfortunately, useable county level data are available only for eleven western states and only these have been mapped.

The 1952 western pattern for Mormons fits the stereotypical geographic image regarding this group. Counties containing the highest category (at least 2000 adherents) are largely confined to the area of "Deseret" extending beyond Utah into southern Idaho, the southwest corner of Wyoming, and eastern Nevada. Other pockets of strength appear in most west coast metropolitan areas and in central Arizona. The 1971 map shows significant changes. First, a much greater proportion of the counties in these western states have been entered, thus giving evidence of Mormon expansion from their core area. Second, although the primary core area remains intact, marked growth is also apparent in urban areas along the West Coast and elsewhere, such as Albuquerque and Denver. All of these areas contain Mormon communities of significant size. It should also be noted that the size limits for the middle category have increased sharply, indicating considerable growth for the Mormons across the entire region.

The percent change map is among the most dramatic in this *Atlas.* The counties in the highest category all register increases in excess of 1000 percent. Many, but not all, of these are counties of new entry. Most importantly, all counties exhibiting 1000 percent or greater change are outside of the traditional Mormon culture hearth surrounding Salt Lake City. Moreover, even the lowest category here could represent growth rates more than twice the national population average. Therefore, the image of the core area as one of declining Mormon strength is erroneous. The shift-share map is strongly similar and again the magnitude of the category limits is almost as significant as the distribution itself. In this portion of the country, the majority of the counties show a marked relative increase in Mormon adherents.

Between 1952 and 1971 the Mormons increased sharply within the relatively constricted area covered by the data. Within these eleven western states they have expanded territorially. By 1971 they cover the entire western region of the nation and in considerably increased numbers. The available national level statistics suggest impressive growth in other parts of the country as well, but little more can be said given the lack of county data for the remaining states.

North American Baptist General Conference

This denomination was founded by German Baptists in Pennsylvania in the 1840's. Its membership remains largely Germanic, while its theology differs little from other 'mainline' Baptist groups. Between 1952 and 1971 they grew from 35,265 to 50,583 adherents, an increase of 43 percent. In 1971 this group had churches in 152 counties, 5 percent of all counties.

The North American Baptists present a curious picture in 1952. Through the Great Lakes region and on the West Coast the group has sizeable numbers in a range of metropolitan centers, but almost entirely without contiguous counties. The only areas in which counties appear in clusters are in the Great Plains, particularly the Dakotas and Kansas. By 1971 this distribution has changed only slightly, with large areas of the Southeast and interior Southwest still devoid of counties containing North American Baptists.

The percent change map is intriguing, as the relatively large urban areas consistently are in the low growth category. The higher growth counties are in the Dakotas cluster, on the West Coast, and also in a few suburban counties adjacent to Detroit, Chicago, Milwaukee and Los Angeles. The shift-share map provides essentially the same pattern of strong relative performance in the northern Plains, indicating a considerable shift away from the group's Pennsylvania origins. The areas in the highest category have all experienced strong relative growth.

The North American Baptists have undergone some numerical growth but relatively little regional shift. They began the period located primarily in the upper Midwest and Great Plains and remain there.

Pentecostal Holiness Church

American Pentecostalism encompasses many revivalist Baptist and Methodist groups. In 1911 the Fire-Baptized Holiness Church, founded in 1898, merged with the Pentecostal Holiness Church, founded in 1899. The Tabernacle Pentecostal Church entered the denomination in 1915. The Church follows Methodist polity and practices divine healing. Between 1952 and 1971 they grew from 41,555 to 89,140 adherents, a 115 percent increase. In 1971 churches were reported in 489 counties, 16 percent of all counties and an increase of 33 percent since 1952.

The 1952 map indicates two major areas of concentration. The larger of these is centered in North and South Carolina and accounts for over 44 percent of the entire denomination. The second cluster is in Oklahoma. The remaining Pentecostal Holiness Churches are scattered throughout the southern states and in relatively weak clusters in California. The most noticeable difference by 1971 is the relative increase in California. The denomination also exhibits geographic expansion in the Pacific Northwest, Colorado, along the fringe of the Great Lakes, and on the northern margins of the Carolina core area, in a band from Virginia through the Washington to Philadelphia urban corridor. However, all of these patterns should be viewed in the context of the fact that even in 1971, the lower limit of the highest adherence category is only 135 people.

The size categories on the change maps show strong relative and absolute growth. The upper limit of the first category of the percent change map (66 percent) is nearly twice that of the national population growth rate. While some of these counties are in the Carolinas, most are in Oklahoma. The high number of counties in the second change category, located in the Carolinas, indicates a strong performance for the denomination in its established core area. The majority of the highest percent change counties are, of course, "new" counties. The same patterns emerge on the shift-share map.

The Pentecostal Holiness Church is typically viewed as a southern religion. This image remains accurate, since by 1971 over 45 percent of the adherents were still located in the Carolinas. While the denomination has not made significant incursions in new regions between 1952 and 1971, it has experienced substantial geographic expansion and absolute growth within its traditional areas.

Presbyterian Church in the United States

Established in 1857 as the United Synod of the Presbyterian Church, this group became the General Assembly of the Presbyterian Church in the Confederate States of America in 1861. Its present name was adopted in 1865. Often called the "Southern Presbyterians" they grew from 745,627 to 1,147,499 adherents between 1952 and 1971, an increase of 54 percent. They reported churches in 1035 counties, 34 percent of all counties in 1971.

This group began as and remains the Southern Presbyterian Church. In 1952 the denomination was located in a continuous distribution in the states of the Confederacy, with scattered counties in the border States of Maryland, West Virginia, Kentucky, Missouri, and Oklahoma. Outside of this historic core area only three counties appear, one each in Pennsylvania, Illinois, and Iowa. By 1971, these three isolated counties had disappeared. New growth has occurred through a process of filling in previously unoccupied territory in the South, most notably in Missouri and Kentucky. For both periods, the primary cluster of adherents extends from Virginia through the Carolinas, with significant concentrations in and around other major population centers in the South, particularly along the coast. It should be noted that in 1952 and 1971 respectively, 500 and 600 people are sufficient to place a county in the highest category on these maps.

The maps of change for this denomination also show that the most rapid growth has taken place outside of the primary core area, but still inside the "old" South. Many of the highest rates of change are in areas of new entry like Missouri, Kentucky, and Florida. These same areas show the greatest increases in the share of total adherence. In both instances the highest rates of absolute and relative increase represent fairly significant growth. Interestingly, on both change maps a significant number of counties in the highest ranks are to be found in a rather small portion of the core area in the southern Piedmont.

Viewed from these data the Presbyterian Church in the U.S. appears to be a strongly regional denomination, within which growth has been both on the margins of and within the center of its traditional core area. As such, the group remains strongly regional and has expanded geographically far less than its counterpart, the United Presbyterian Church in the U.S.A.

Reformed Church in America

The Reformed Churches, i.e. European Calvinist Churches, arrived in New Amsterdam in the early 1600's. Doctrinal disputes led to the separate formation of the Dutch Reformed Church in North America in the 1790's. In the 1850's it absorbed several small Reformed groups from midwestern states, and adopted its present name in 1867. It has a modified presbyterian form of polity. Between 1952 and 1971 this denomination grew from 194,157 to 370,509 adherents, an increase of 91 percent. In 1971 it reported churches in 203 counties, 7 percent of all counties, representing an increase of 34 percent since 1952.

As the denominational history would suggest, the 1952 map shows areas of strength in both the Northeast and the Midwest. The more extensive of these is largely in New York, running from New York City through the Hudson and Mohawk valleys to the Great Lakes. Smaller clusters of counties are located in western Michigan and in Iowa. Although New York contained more than one-third of the denomination's adherents, the locational balance of the denomination is illustrated by the fact that the two largest

individual counties were located in Michigan. By 1971 new clusters have developed in Florida, Oklahoma, and New Mexico, as well as several midwestern metropolitan areas, including Chicago and Detroit. This changing distribution suggests a relative decline in older areas. Accordingly, by 1971 the proportion of adherents found in New York had dropped to 25 percent.

The two change maps clearly depict these shifts. The lower category on the percent change map includes rates as high as 73 percent. Predictably, most of these instances are in the traditional power base of the denomination in upstate New York. Conversely, most of the midwestern counties are in the two higher change categories, with the highest growth rates frequently indicating counties of new entry for the denomination. The shift-share map depicts essentially the same pattern. The group increased its share of total religious adherence even in its lowest category shift-share counties, and made substantial gains, primarily in its newer midwestern and far western counties. The New York area generally displays more modest relative performance.

Despite these shifts, the Reformed Church remains a fairly small, highly ethnic denomination, with multiregional, but highly selective, geographic coverage. Its impressive change rate between 1952 and 1971 should not obscure the fact that the group is located in less than ten percent of the counties and numbers less than half a million people.

Seventh-Day Adventist

Following the ideas of William Miller, Adventism focuses upon the hoped for second coming of Christ. The Seventh-Day Adventists emerged in the 1840's and 1850's, adopting their name in 1860. This is a conservative, evangelical version of the Baptist faith, practicing adult immersion. Between 1952 and 1971 they grew from 252,554 to 536,082 adherents, an increase of 112 percent. In 1971 there were Adventist churches in 1624 counties, 53 percent of all counties.

The 1952 distribution of the Seventh-Day Adventists is one of the few patterns in the *Atlas* with a distinctively western orientation. All three size categories could easily represent single congregations, as the lower limit for the highest one is less than 100 adherents. The apparent core of strength for the denomination is in an area running from the Pacific Northwest, through California, and into central Arizona. Secondary clusters of strength are in Michigan, upstate New York, and along the northeastern seacoast. Otherwise, the 1952 pattern is rather diffuse. The 1971 pattern is slightly changed. Western strength is still clearly apparent and has increased somewhat in the Rocky Mountain states, excluding the Mormon areas of Utah and Idaho. In the Northeast the same areas of relative strength appear, with some increases in the mid-Atlantic states and central Florida. Since the upper limit of the lowest category represents barely 50 persons, the Southeast and the states from Texas northward contain only a thin scattering of Seventh-Day Adventists.

The percent change map shows a picture of substantial increase in areas of new entry. While relatively few high growth rate counties are on the West Coast, many are in the western interior. Other instances of the highest growth rates are scattered across the Southeast and in the urban corridor from Washington north along the coast. Elsewhere, low and moderate growth rates are intermingled without a distinct pattern. The shift-share map is rather similar. Counties of strong relative performance are scattered from coast to coast, although they are somewhat more common in areas of smaller absolute numbers. In other words, such areas include the Southeast and the mountain states but not the western coastal region.

This group is present throughout the entire country, but in most instances the actual numbers of adherents is quite small, usually less than 150 persons per county. Thus, despite a nationwide pattern, the Seventh-Day Adventists remain what might be termed a national sect rather than either a national or regional denomination.

Seventh-Day Baptist
General Conference

Initially known as Sabatarian Baptists, this group is English in origin and was organized in America in 1672 at Newport, Rhode Island. They place a strong emphasis upon individual religious liberty and adhere to congregational polity. The General Conference is essentially a voluntary federation of churches. Between 1952 and 1971 they experienced a slight decrease of 4 percent, from 6,435 to 5,178 adherents. In 1971 churches were reported in 45 counties, less than 2 percent of all counties.

This very small group is unique among the denominations represented in the *Atlas,* as they have experienced a decline in adherents. In 1952 they were scattered randomly over some 46 counties in 20 states, with no clusters of more than three contiguous counties in any one place. Outside Allegany County in upstate New York, which contained 15.6 percent of the group's adherents, the denomination's distribution was very diffuse. The 1971 distribution involves much the same coast-to-coast random pattern, while the relative contribution of Allegany County had slipped to only 11.4 percent.

The maps of change depict a very random pattern. Counties that have experienced absolute and relative declines are found in the same regions with, and often in close proximity to, counties that have grown. As a consequence, there seems to be little consistent pattern of change on a regional basis.

The Seventh-Day Baptists are a very small and shrinking denomination. They do not appear consistently in any area outside of upstate New York, and are in relatively small, and in some cases decreasing numbers, even there.

Southern Baptist Convention

The Southern Baptist Convention was founded in 1845. The division between northern and southern Baptists focused not only upon the slavery issue, but on the Southerners' desire for a stronger denominational body than was desired in the North. Today, the Southern Baptist Convention is the largest American Protestant denomination. Between 1952 and 1971 it grew from 8,121,069 to 14,488,634 adherents, or 78 percent. In 1971 it reported churches in 2212 counties, 72 percent of all counties and an increase of 24 percent since 1952.

The Southern Baptist Convention exhibits one of the most dramatic patterns of any group portrayed in this *Atlas.* A comparison of the 1952 and 1971 total adherents maps shows a strong expansion into the northern states. In both periods the counties in the highest category are solidly southern from coast to coast. Nonetheless, by 1971 a few of the highest category counties appear in metropolitan areas of the upper Midwest (for example, Cincinnati, Columbus, Detroit, Chicago) and in some western areas (for example, Denver, Seattle). An obvious expansion has occurred throughout virtually all portions of the northern states. Moreover, the number of adherents per county for this group is higher than those for most Protestant groups. The lowest category for Southern Baptists could include counties possessing several moderate sized congregations.

The change maps depict this expansion most graphically. The top category of percent change represents increases of more than 180 percent. These counties are located almost exclusively outside of the South, the only significant exceptions being in southern Florida and the Mississippi delta. The areas of highest change rates cover the western states and are scattered throughout the Northeast. The map of shift-share shows a similar pattern. The greatest upward shifts are found in the western states, the Midwest and Northeast, all of which are areas of new entry for the Southern Baptists. Conversely, the traditional southern core area of the group contains almost none of the counties with the sharpest increases in the Southern Baptist share of total adherence. However, for this denomination even the middle shift-share category includes counties within which the group has increased it's share of membership to a considerable degree.

In summary, the Southern Baptist Convention has made dramatic increases outside of its traditional "home" territory. Although the group continues to possess its greatest strength in the Old South, it has expanded between 1952 and 1971 to become a truly national denomination.

Unitarian Universalist Association

The Unitarian Universalist Association was formed by a 1961 merger of the American Unitarian Association and the Universalist Church of America. The Unitarians began as a reform group within Congregationalism in the 1770's and became autonomous in 1825. The Universalists stem from an English movement in the 1770's and were organized in America by the 1790's. This is one of the least doctrinal groups in the American Protestant spectrum. Between 1952 and 1971 they grew from 159,904 adherents to 194,733, a 22 percent increase. In 1971 they had churches in 520 counties, 17 percent of all counties and an increase of 42 percent since 1952.

The historic identification of Unitarianism and Universalism with New England is clearly depicted on the 1952 map. While these groups reported adherents in all regions of the country, strong clusters of high category contiguous counties are almost exclusively restricted to the six New England states and upstate New York. By 1971 the number of high category counties in northern New England and New York State has diminished. Moreover, the merged denomination has strong counties throughout the Washington, D.C., to New York corridor, and in metropolitan counties in all regions of the nation.

These shifts are easily discerned on the two, virtually identical, change maps. Low category shift-share and percent change counties blanket most of New England and New York State, as well as previously established locations in other regions of the nation. In most of these counties, which constitute over a third of the denomination's counties, the group has experienced relative decline. The high shift-share and percent change locations are nearly all counties of new entry and are uniformly outside the old home territory.

The Unitarian Universalists have made a substantial shift away from New England. Statistical evidence of this shift is provided by the percent of adherents located in Massachusetts, which slipped from 31 percent of the denomination in 1952, to slightly over 20 percent in 1971. In the process of dispersion, this group has become relatively unique among Protestant groups, possessing a metropolitan character most resembling that of Catholics and Jews.

areas of strength remain in New England, upper New York state, New Jersey, Pennsylvania, Michigan, Ohio, and Indiana.

The change maps provide a mixed pattern. The lower limit of the category representing the highest growth rate is a relatively low 32 percent, indicating modest growth. High growth rate counties are not as common for the UCC in the Northeast as are high category adherence counties in either 1952 or 1971. However, more high category change counties are in the Northeast than elsewhere in the nation. Formerly small areas experiencing high growth rates are found in the Great Plains, Rocky Mountain states, and in Florida. The shift-share map must be interpreted in light of the fact that only the highest category represents counties within which the UCC has retained its position relative to total religious growth. Such areas are most common in the Northeast, typically in non-metropolitan areas such as upstate New York, central Pennsylvania, eastern Ohio, and downstate Illinois. Fewer areas of the highest category appear in the West and Florida than on the preceding map, indicating that relative growth was less pronounced than absolute growth. Nonetheless, the pervasive image is of relative decline. That pattern is common in all areas where the UCC is present.

Between 1952 and 1971 the merged denomination, The United Church of Christ, has been characterized by stability in both its numbers and location. This stability has resulted in considerable relative decline within the areas of traditional strength. The UCC has shown little movement toward becoming a national denomination.

United Church of Christ and Congregational Christian Churches

The United Church of Christ was formed by a 1961 merger of the Congregational Christian Churches and the Evangelical and Reformed Church. Both denominations were products of mergers in 1931 and 1934 respectively. A group of about 300 Congregational churches did not enter the 1961 merger and remained a separate denomination. They have been included in the 1971 data here in order to maintain comparability with the combined 1952 statistics for the Congregational Christian Churches and the Evangelical and Reformed Church. Between 1952 and 1971 the UCC and CC churches grew from 2,013,935 to 2,411,478 adherents, a 20 percent increase. In 1971 they reported churches in 1296 counties, 42 percent of all counties, and a 7 percent decrease since 1952.

Congregationalism is typically associated with New England. However, as a result of nineteenth century migration and twentieth century denominational mergers, both the 1952 and 1971 United Church of Christ distributions blanket the Northeast and upper Midwest. UCC churches thin rapidly west of the Mississippi, with additional strong concentrations in 1952 only on the West Coast, in North Carolina (formerly Christian churches), and in Texas (formerly Evangelical and Reformed churches). There are few changes in this distribution by 1971, with the UCC still strikingly absent south of the Mason-Dixon line. The major

United Methodist Church and Evangelical Church of North America

The United Methodist Church resulted from two successive mergers, the first occurring in 1939. That merger was a reunion of three major Methodist groups that had divided over both doctrinal matters and the slavery issue. In 1968 the Methodist Church merged with the Evangelical United Brethren. A small group of EUB's objected to that merger and joined with the Holiness Methodist Church forming the Evangelical Church of North America. These several groups have been added together in both the 1971 and 1952 data in order to maintain comparability. These denominations grew from 9,512,669 to 11,523,749 adherents between 1952 and 1971, a modest 21 percent increase. They reported churches in 2955 counties in 1971, 96 percent of all counties.

The distribution of United Methodists is clearly a national one, and in many ways mirrors the distribution of the United States population in both 1952 and 1971. While there are a few areas in the South and the Mountain West without Methodists in 1952, many of those areas, particularly in the eastern half of the country have been filled in by 1971. In both 1952 and 1971 the areas of strongest concentration are in the northeastern quarter of the country, forming an arc from Boston to St. Louis, with significant secondary clusters throughout the southeast from the Carolina

Piedmont to central Texas. By 1971 substantial strength had emerged in western states as well.

The percent change map displays a very different pattern. The highest growth rate areas are primarily outside of the Northeast. The cut-off point for the highest category here is well below the national population growth rate. The areas in which the rate of increase is greatest are largely in the western half of the country, surprisingly including some areas of the Great Plains, an area frequently characterized by either population stability or decline. Other instances of notable expansion are in Florida and south Texas, which also appear as areas of United Methodist strength on the distribution maps. Exceptions to this pattern of expansion outside of the "core" area are in a band from upstate New York through Michigan to Wisconsin. Conversely, areas of decline (the lowest category here) are scattered throughout the northeastern area of concentration, and in areas of less traditional strength in the interior South (Arkansas, Missouri, and Tennessee). The shift-share map for United Methodists shows a strong bias to the interior western sections of the country (as opposed to the Northeast), with isolated spots of relative growth scattered through the southern states. This group, like many other larger Protestant denominations, failed to keep pace with rapid increases in total population in southern California and Florida.

In summary, the United Methodists were already a national denomination by 1952, and between 1952 and 1971, increased their presence in various regions of the nation. Their change pattern depicts growth in areas of traditional strength and areas that are new for them.

United Presbyterian Church in the U.S.A.

The larger branch of American Presbyterianism was founded in the early 1700's by Scotch-Irish Calvinists (Covenanters) and English Presbyterians. It experienced numerous schisms and unions during the 19th century. In 1906 it merged with a substantial portion of the Cumberland Presbyterian churches. A 1958 merger of the Presbyterian Church in the U.S.A. and the United Presbyterian Church of North America reunited old light and new light churches, and different ethnic churches. (The southern branch of the church and a still independent Cumberland Presbyterian group did not enter this merger.) Between 1952 and 1971 they grew from 2,670,167 to 3,546,941 adherents, a 33 percent increase. In 1971 churches were reported in 1857 counties, 60 percent of all counties.

This denomination still reflects some of the effects of the split among Presbyterians that occurred over one hundred years ago. The original core area extending from the mid-Atlantic states westward to Illinois is still the dominant component of the national pattern. However, in both 1952 and 1971 a considerable shift to the West is also apparent, particularly along the coast. A limited expansion has occurred in the South, largely in the border states and the Piedmont, as well as in Florida. However, most

counties in these areas are in the lower size categories and therefore represent relatively small numbers of people. Consequently, this denomination may still accurately be described as the "Northern" Presbyterian Church.

The maps depicting both percent change and change in the share of total religious adherence are not as strikingly different from the maps of absolute incidence as is the case for many other major denominations. Most of the highest growth rates are in the West and in certain areas of the South, such as central Texas, Kentucky, and Florida. However, a significant number of counties with the highest growth rates are in the older northeastern core area. Overall, the rates of change throughout are modest. The lowest category of the percent change map and the lowest two categories of the shift-share map all indicate declines.

In summary, the United Presbyterians can be characterized as a group that has experienced some movement from its original core area. Although the group has made some notable incursions into the South, it is not strongly represented in that region by 1971. However, as a result of successive mergers, and a significant growth rate it is clearly in the process of becoming a national denomination.

Wisconsin Evangelical Lutheran Synod

American Lutheranism reflects various divisions both within and between formerly European national churches. The First German Lutheran Synod of Wisconsin was formed in 1850. In 1918 it merged with groups from several near-by states to become the "Joint Synod of Wisconsin and Other States." Its present name was adopted in 1959. This is a conservative brand of Lutheranism, and has remained outside the ALC and LCA because of the doctrinal heterogeneity of those groups. Between 1952 and 1971 it grew from 318,642 to 381,920 adherents, a 21 percent increase. In 1971 churches were reported in 352 counties, 12 percent of all counties, representing an increase of 42 percent since 1952.

In 1952 the state of Wisconsin contained over 58 percent of the Wisconsin Lutherans. A highly compact region of contiguous counties extended south to Chicago and west thru southern Minnesota. The largest single concentration of Wisconsin Lutherans was in Milwaukee. Outside of the upper Midwest, the only other area of strength is in Arizona. Several changes occurred in 1971. Small numbers of adherents have emerged in isolated counties in the southern and eastern states. Strong clusters of counties fill the metropolitan areas along the West Coast. However, the primary core area, the state of Wisconsin, remains the dominant feature. In fact, that state's share of the denomination's adherence increased to over 68 percent in 1971.

The highest category on both change maps identify "new" counties for the denomination. However, given the strong increase experienced within Wisconsin, the impression of strong growth in marginal areas is somewhat misleading. This increase is shown by strong shift-share performances within the original core region. Areas of relative decline were located in peripheral areas such as the Great Plains and Arizona.

The Wisconsin Lutherans exhibit a unique pattern of change for the period 1952 to 1971. While the historic core area grew to contain an ever greater proportion of the national Church, substantial geographic dispersion also occurred. Thus, in a numeric sense the denomination became more highly regionalized while in a spatial sense it became significantly less regional.

All Denominations: National Patterns

The focus of this *Atlas* upon individual denominations has involved the recurrent theme of religious regionalism. Most American religious groups are relatively small, both in numbers and geographic extent, and most can be traced to specific geographic circumstances of origin and development. It is therefore important, before examining patterns of aggregate religion for the period, to consider the degree of national scope of individual denominations and their broader denominational families.

First, there are at least three individual denominations that are truely national in character, Roman Catholics, United Methodists, and Southern Baptists. In 1971, they reported adherents in 92 percent, 96 percent, and 72 percent of all counties respectively. Catholicism is, of course, the largest single Christian group in the nation. The Southern Baptists and United Methodists are each more than twice the size of any other Protestant group. These three denominations are also national in the sense that each exerts significant cultural force in at least one region of the country, and each has substantial numbers of adherents in more than one region.

In 1971 the Southern Baptists were both the largest single Protestant denomination and the leader of the largest family of Protestant denominations. That family includes of course, the American Baptist Churches in the U.S.A., essentially the northern wing of the family, and a host of smaller Baptist groups, including the North American Baptist General Conference, the Baptist General Conference, the Seventh-Day Baptists and others. Perhaps the most significant emergent member of this family is the Seventh-Day Adventists. They have impressive national coverage but are not yet culturally dominant in any one region. The Baptist family is completed by the Mennonites, various Bretheren groups, and the Moravians.

The United Methodists may also be viewed as the flagship of a broader family of denominations that constitute a national faith. The Church of the Nazarene is an important theological and geographic extension of Methodism. Like the Seventh-Day Adventists, the Nazarenes have broad geographic coverage, but also are not a salient cultural factor in any one region. They are very likely an emerging national denomination. Thus, the United Methodists, the Nazarenes, a number of smaller Methodist denominations such as the Free Methodist Church, and one major group not included in these data, the Assemblies of God, represent a major national religious grouping.

It should also be noted that the Roman Catholic church has eclipsed the distribution of the Episcopal Church. Both denominations are multiregional and have historically strong concentrations in the Northeast and on the Atlantic Coast. Episcopalianism is yet another Protestant group that is national in scope, but is not a cultural force even in its areas of highest density. However, unlike the Seventh-Day Adventists and the Nazarenes, both of which grew impressively between 1952 and 1971, the Episcopalians exhibit relative decline.

Three denominations seem to be multi-regional but not national. However, two of them, when combined with other groups in their denominational families, can be viewed as national religions. In 1971 the Lutheran Church-Missouri Synod was present in 54 percent of all counties and in all regions, though it is clearly weak in the South. Its distribution is complemented by the ALC and LCA much like the pieces of a jigsaw puzzle. These three major Lutheran groups have an impressive combined national coverage.

A similar situation prevails in the Presbyterian family. Through its several mergers, the United Presbyterian Church U.S.A. has major strength in all regions except the South. If the Presbyterian Church in the U.S., the southern wing of the Church, is combined with the United Presbyterians, a genuinely national Church emerges. Moreover, the Christian Reformed Church and the Reformed Church in America are both part of the Presbyterian tradition, and serve to add smaller pockets of strength to the national coverage of that denominational network.

Finally, the United Church of Christ is also multi-regional, with coverage in the Northeast and upper Midwest, and metropolitan areas elsewhere in the nation. However, the diverse theological traditions that have entered this denomination through successive organizational mergers make it difficult to speak of a denominational family in the historic sense. Some of the smaller Evangelical denominations might be considered as part of the extended UCC family. Obviously, the smaller Reformed groups have a theological affinity with both the UCC and Presbyterianism. Should the proposed merger between the UCC and the Disciples of Christ be completed, the denomination will clearly have national stature.

Unfortunately, these data do not allow an assessment of the role of Mormonism, for which only western states information is available. Further, there is no information in this *Atlas* on the Assemblies of God, limited data for Churches of God, (i.e. only the Anderson and Cleveland Churches of God), and none for Black denominations. As already noted, the Assemblies are an extension of Methodism, just as the Churches of Christ and Churches of God are forms of the Baptist faith. It is likely that data for these groups would illustrate additional national coverage for these denominational families. It is nonetheless clear that the data in these maps provide ample support for both regional and national perceptions of the nature of American denomination.

Having considered these major family groupings, we may next examine the combined patterns of national religion that they create. The 1952 and 1971 maps for all denominations provide the aggregate pictures for the more than 80 percent of reported religious adherence for the two periods contained in this *Atlas*.

These two maps might easily serve as surrogates for population density maps of the United States in their respective years. In other words, while the individual denominational maps depict a diversity of patterns, the pattern of aggregate religion is closely tied to the distributions of the general population in both 1952 and 1971.

Similarly, the map depicting percent change in total adherents appears to correlate strongly with general patterns of population change. The highest category of change has a lower limit of 52 percent, indicating that one third of the counties experienced significant growth in religious adherents during the period. Many of the counties in this category are located in the "Sun Belt," where high religious growth rates coincide with dynamic economic growth and substantial in-migration. Typical areas are the Gulf Coast and Florida, urban counties in the Piedmont, Tennessee and Texas, population centers in Colorado and Arizona, and west coast metropolitan communities. In the North and East such counties are less common and are mostly associated with urban configurations of major proportions, such as the corridors from New York to Washington, D.C. and around the southern Great Lakes. The lowest category here could include religious growth rates up to 18 percent, about half that of the national population growth rate. However, it is important to recall that large numbers of counties, particularly in more rural agricultural areas, declined in population during this period. It is not surprising that this category appears frequently in such areas as the Great Plains, the upper Great Lakes region, Appalachia, and the rural Southeast. This category is also common in much of upstate New York, New England, and in the mountain states where population levels have been relatively stable. In sum, the pattern of change in total religious adherence is highly consistent with patterns of general population change in the county for the period from 1950 to 1970.

This shift-share map differs from all others in this *Atlas*, as the adjusted white United States census population statistics have been used to calculate the index. Thus, this map shows the shift in all religious groups *vis-a-vis* population change. The shift-share category limits, rather than surrounding a value of 1.0, are somewhat higher. This supports the idea that a major revival of religion occurred during this period, because aggregate patterns show consistent increases across the country. However, the most important aspect of the change maps is the difference in percent change in religious adherence and the performance of religion relative to population change (shift-share). Many of the West Coast areas exhibiting high religious growth are in the lower shift-share category. Conversely, within the Great Plains and upper Midwest, which have more modest religious growth rates, the religious groups outdistanced population change. The reasons for these variations in the two maps are not readily apparent. Nonetheless, it is clear that there are strong regional differences in terms of the relative ability of religious groups to keep pace with total population growth. Clearly, in some areas already noted for their secular tendencies, religious groups have been less successful than in some others that have been noted to have more sectarian cultures. These differences illustrate the persistence of religion as an important component of regional culture in America.

Maps

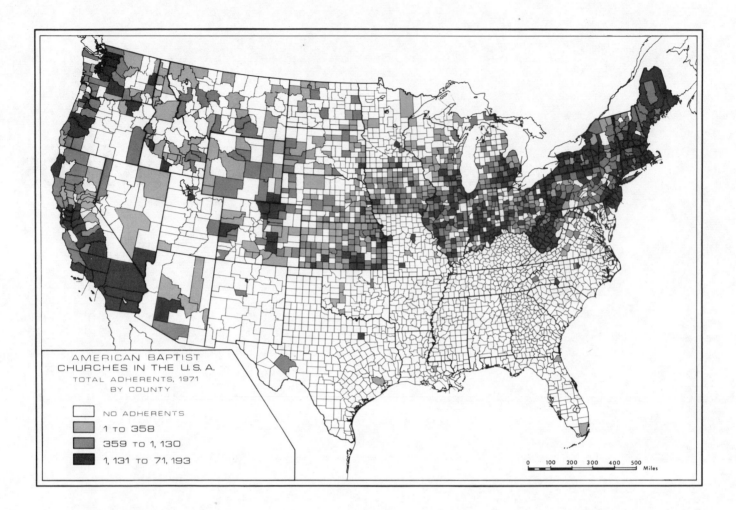

AMERICAN BAPTIST
CHURCHES IN THE U.S.A.
TOTAL ADHERENTS, 1971
BY COUNTY

NO ADHERENTS
1 TO 358
359 TO 1,130
1,131 TO 71,193

0 100 200 300 400 500 Miles

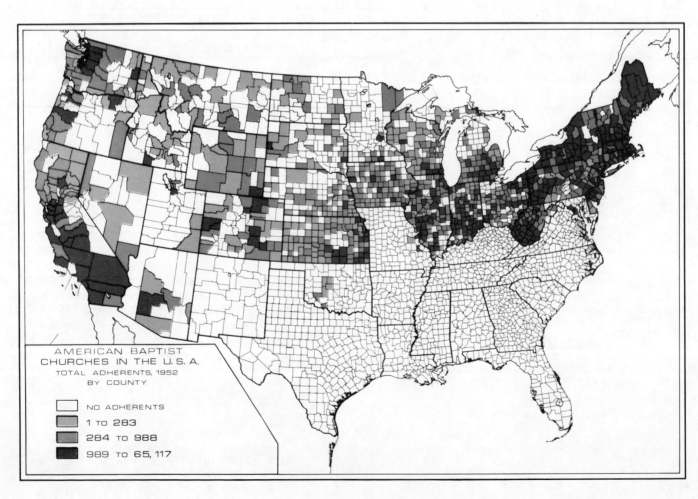

AMERICAN BAPTIST
CHURCHES IN THE U.S.A.
TOTAL ADHERENTS, 1952
BY COUNTY

NO ADHERENTS
1 TO 283
284 TO 988
989 TO 65,117

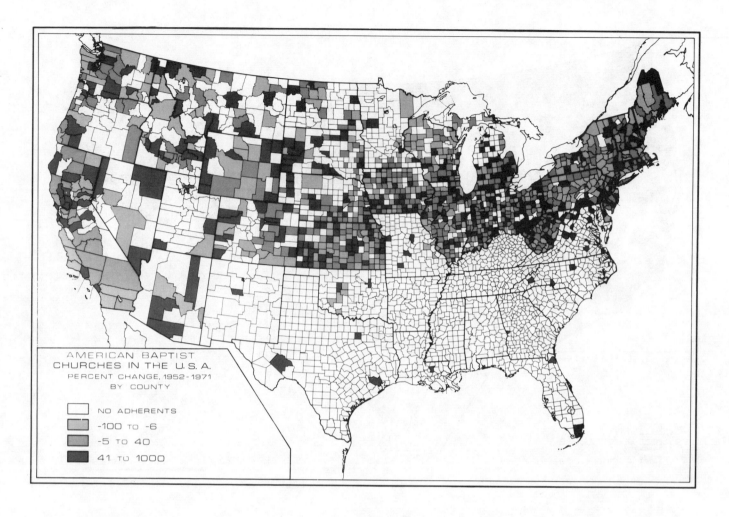

AMERICAN BAPTIST
CHURCHES IN THE U.S.A.
PERCENT CHANGE, 1952-1971
BY COUNTY

NO ADHERENTS
-100 TO -6
-5 TO 40
41 TO 1000

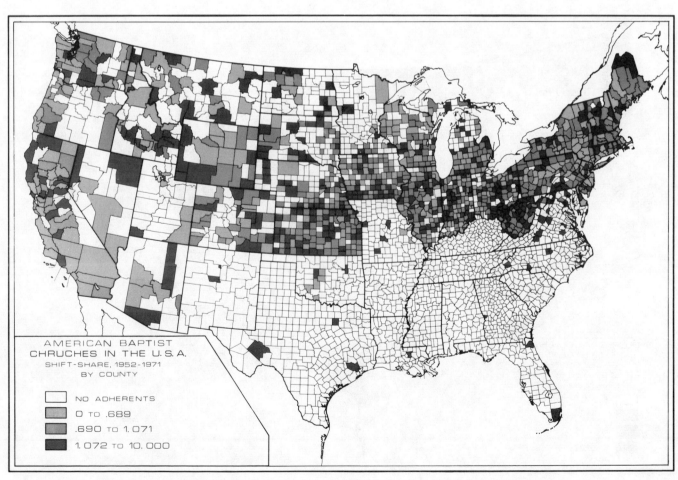

AMERICAN BAPTIST
CHRUCHES IN THE U.S.A.
SHIFT-SHARE, 1952-1971
BY COUNTY

NO ADHERENTS
0 TO .689
.690 TO 1.071
1.072 TO 10.000

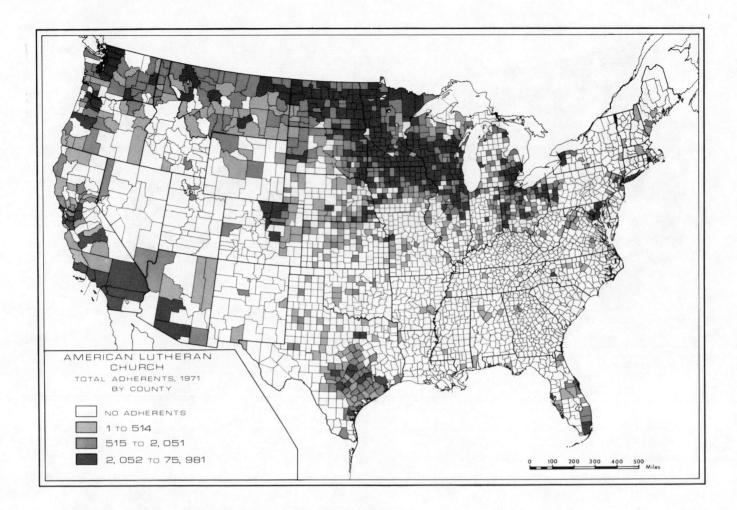

AMERICAN LUTHERAN
CHURCH
TOTAL ADHERENTS, 1971
BY COUNTY

NO ADHERENTS
1 TO 514
515 TO 2, 051
2, 052 TO 75, 981

0   100   200   300   400   500
Miles

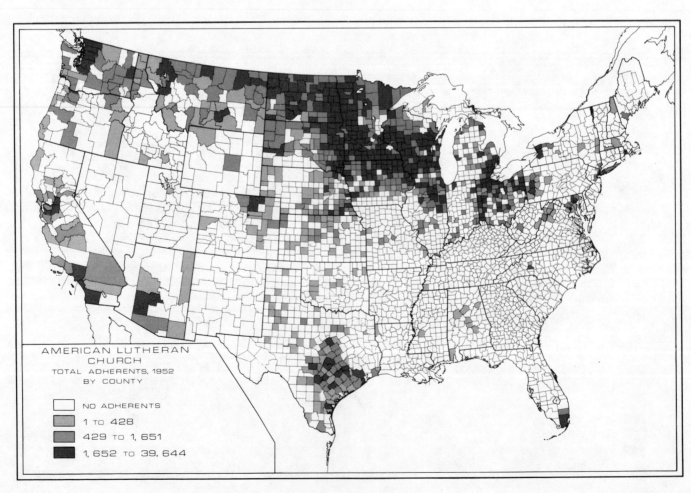

AMERICAN LUTHERAN
CHURCH
TOTAL ADHERENTS, 1952
BY COUNTY

NO ADHERENTS
1 TO 428
429 TO 1, 651
1, 652 TO 39, 644

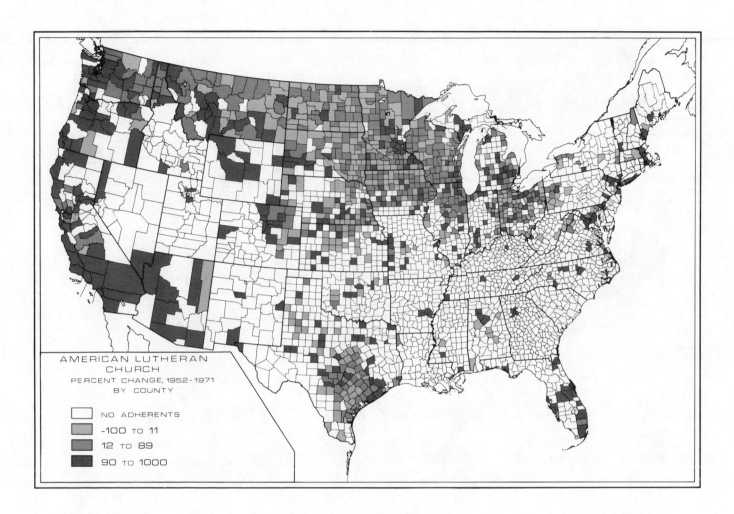

AMERICAN LUTHERAN
CHURCH
PERCENT CHANGE, 1952-1971
BY COUNTY

     NO ADHERENTS
     -100 TO 11
     12 TO 89
     90 TO 1000

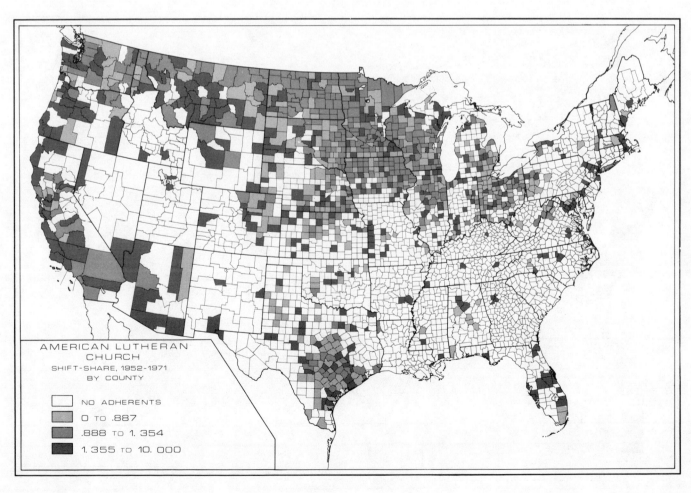

AMERICAN LUTHERAN
CHURCH
SHIFT-SHARE, 1952-1971
BY COUNTY

     NO ADHERENTS
     0 TO .887
     .888 TO 1. 354
     1. 355 TO 10. 000

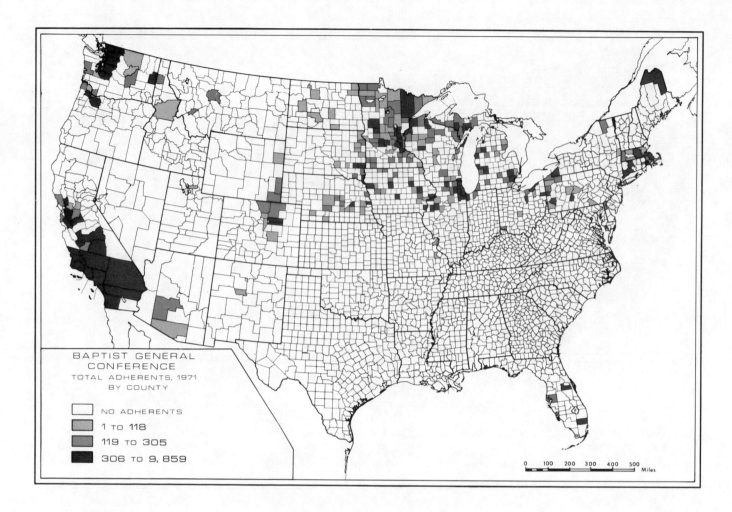

BAPTIST GENERAL
CONFERENCE
TOTAL ADHERENTS, 1971
BY COUNTY

NO ADHERENTS
1 TO 118
119 TO 305
306 TO 9,859

0 100 200 300 400 500
Miles

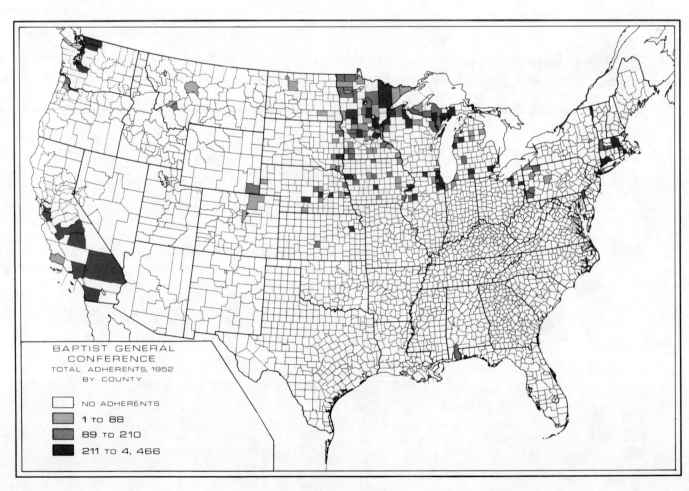

BAPTIST GENERAL
CONFERENCE
TOTAL ADHERENTS, 1952
BY COUNTY

NO ADHERENTS
1 TO 88
89 TO 210
211 TO 4,466

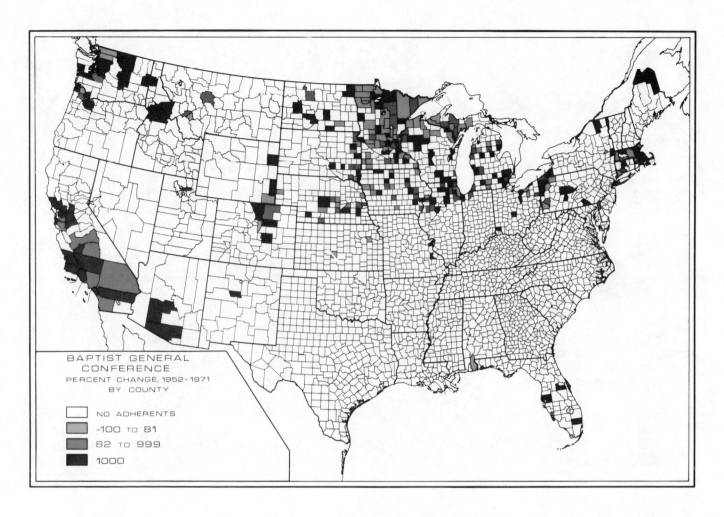

BAPTIST GENERAL
CONFERENCE
PERCENT CHANGE, 1952-1971
BY COUNTY

NO ADHERENTS
-100 TO 81
82 TO 999
1000

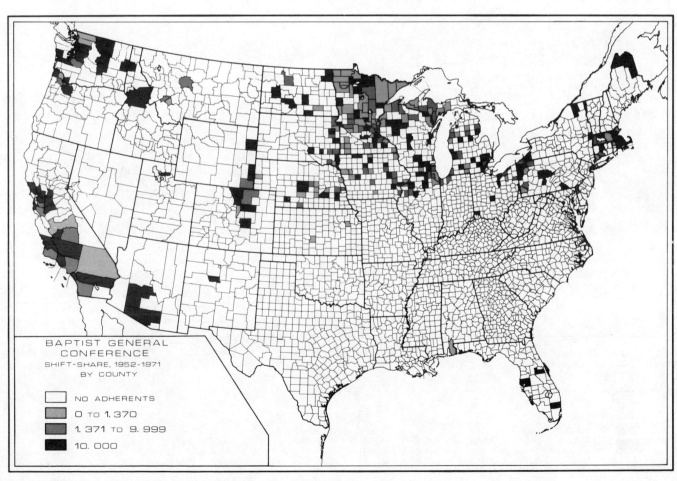

BAPTIST GENERAL
CONFERENCE
SHIFT-SHARE, 1952-1971
BY COUNTY

NO ADHERENTS
0 TO 1.370
1.371 TO 9.999
10.000

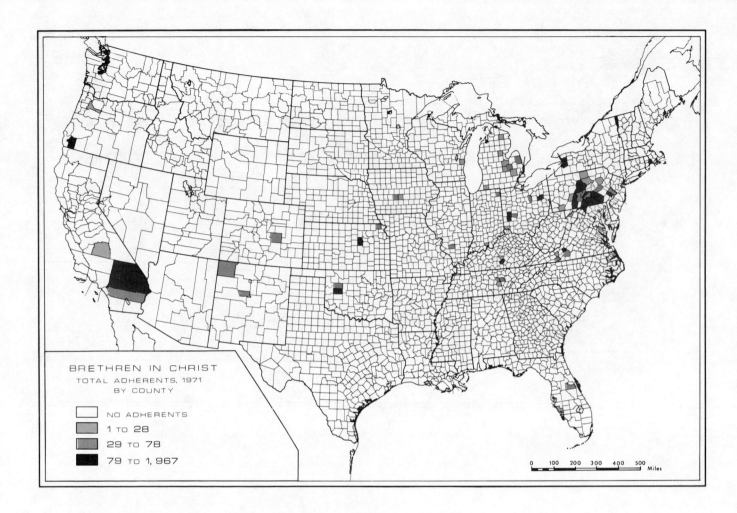

BRETHREN IN CHRIST
TOTAL ADHERENTS, 1971
BY COUNTY

NO ADHERENTS
1 TO 28
29 TO 78
79 TO 1,967

0 100 200 300 400 500
Miles

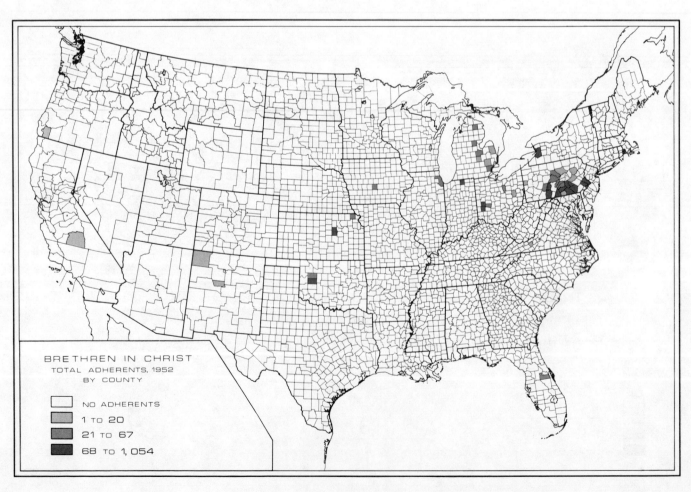

BRETHREN IN CHRIST
TOTAL ADHERENTS, 1952
BY COUNTY

NO ADHERENTS
1 TO 20
21 TO 67
68 TO 1,054

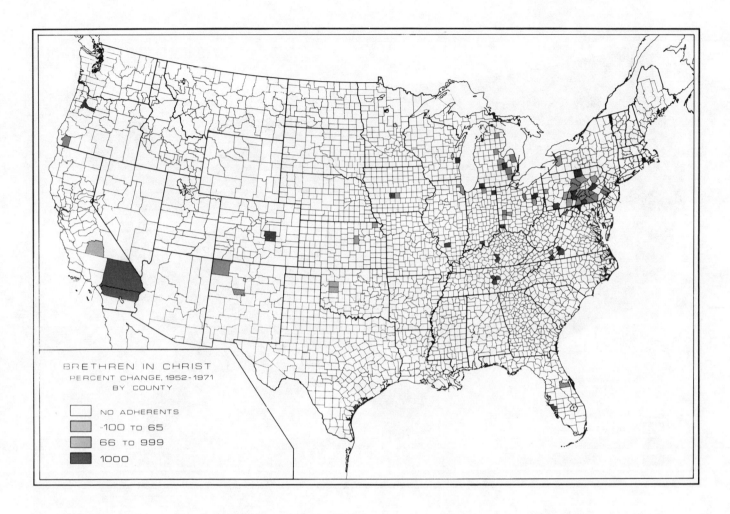

BRETHREN IN CHRIST
PERCENT CHANGE, 1952-1971
BY COUNTY

NO ADHERENTS
-100 TO 65
66 TO 999
1000

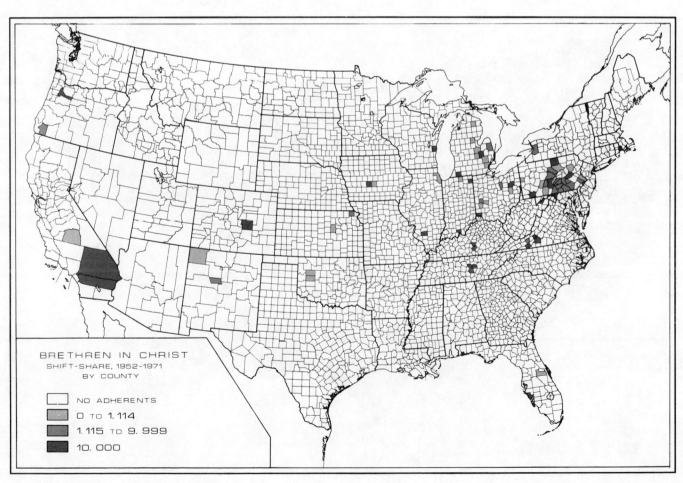

BRETHREN IN CHRIST
SHIFT-SHARE, 1952-1971
BY COUNTY

NO ADHERENTS
0 TO 1.114
1.115 TO 9.999
10.000

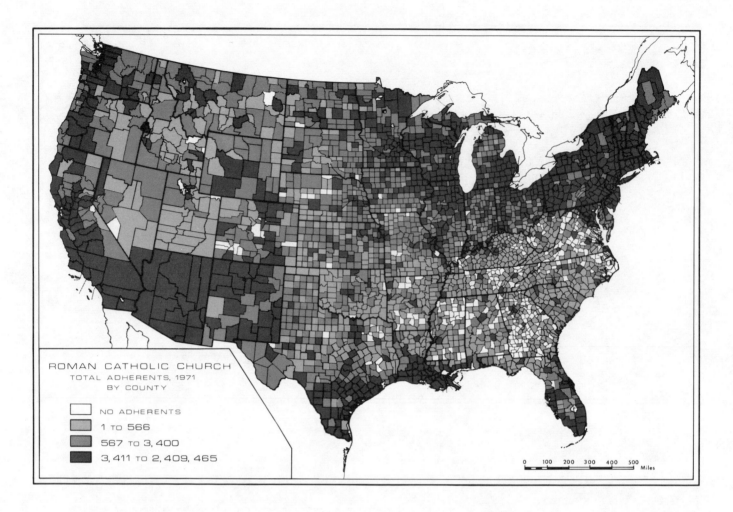

ROMAN CATHOLIC CHURCH
TOTAL ADHERENTS, 1971
BY COUNTY

NO ADHERENTS
1 TO 566
567 TO 3,400
3,411 TO 2,409,465

0 100 200 300 400 500 Miles

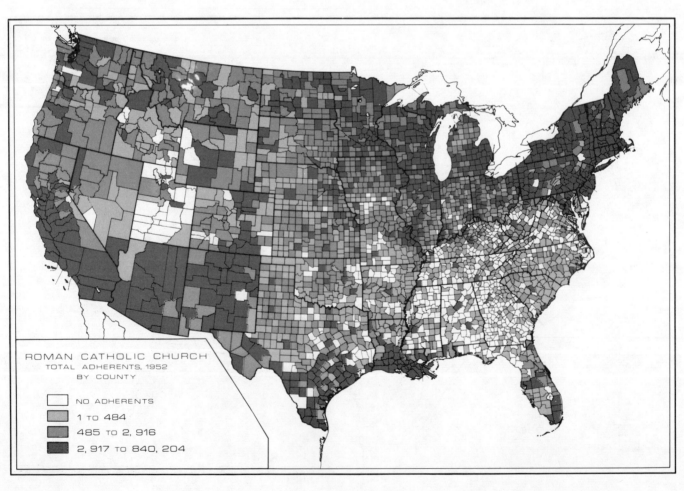

ROMAN CATHOLIC CHURCH
TOTAL ADHERENTS, 1952
BY COUNTY

NO ADHERENTS
1 TO 484
485 TO 2,916
2,917 TO 840,204

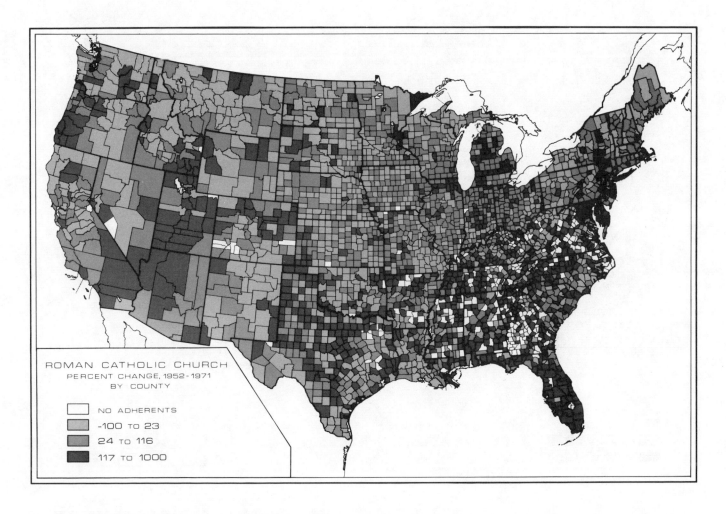

ROMAN CATHOLIC CHURCH
PERCENT CHANGE, 1952-1971
BY COUNTY

- NO ADHERENTS
- -100 TO 23
- 24 TO 116
- 117 TO 1000

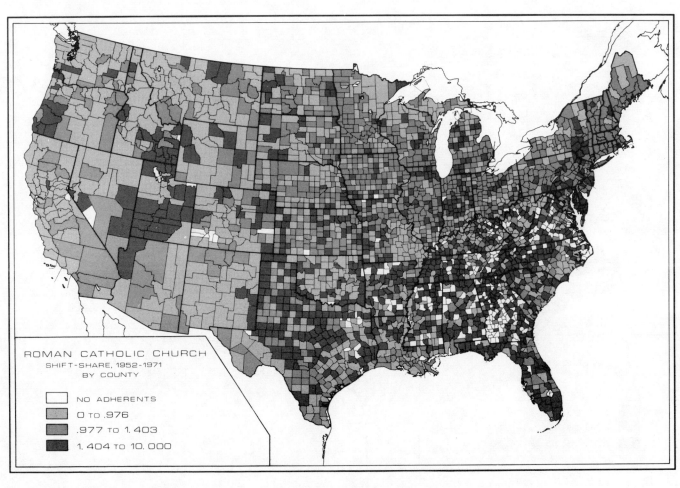

ROMAN CATHOLIC CHURCH
SHIFT-SHARE, 1952-1971
BY COUNTY

- NO ADHERENTS
- 0 TO .976
- .977 TO 1.403
- 1.404 TO 10.000

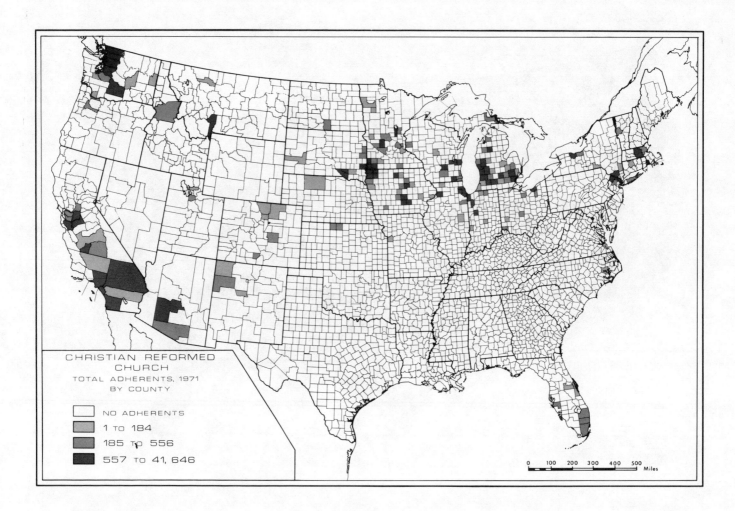

CHRISTIAN REFORMED
CHURCH
TOTAL ADHERENTS, 1971
BY COUNTY

NO ADHERENTS
1 TO 184
185 TO 556
557 TO 41, 646

0   100   200   300   400   500
Miles

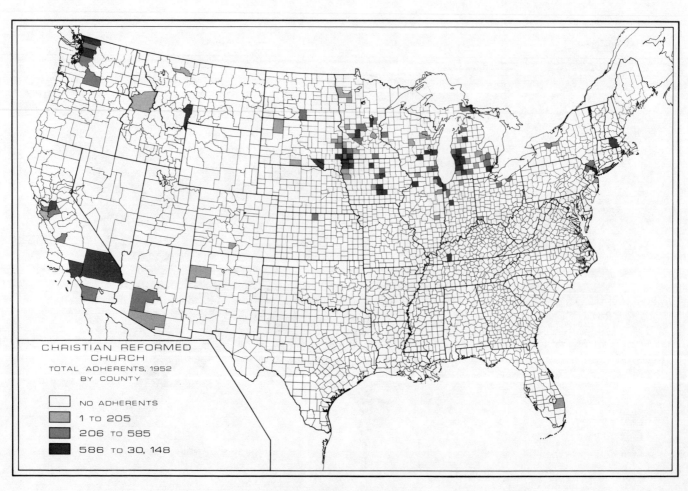

CHRISTIAN REFORMED
CHURCH
TOTAL ADHERENTS, 1952
BY COUNTY

NO ADHERENTS
1 TO 205
206 TO 585
586 TO 30, 148

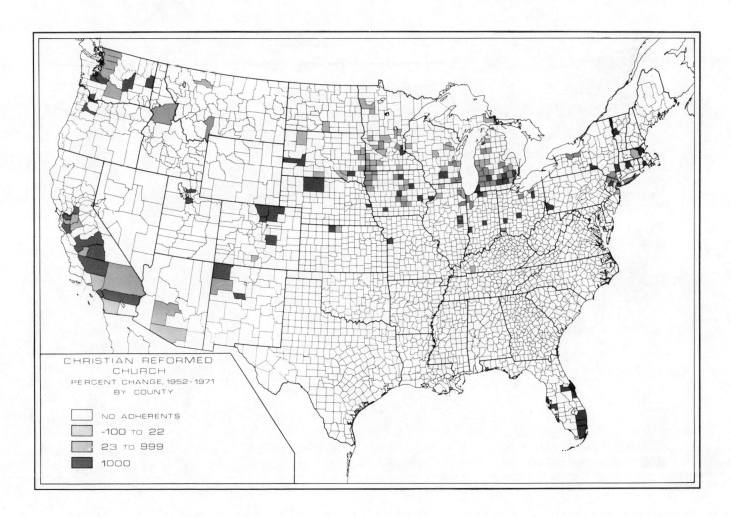

CHRISTIAN REFORMED
CHURCH
PERCENT CHANGE, 1952-1971
BY COUNTY

NO ADHERENTS
-100 TO 22
23 TO 999
1000

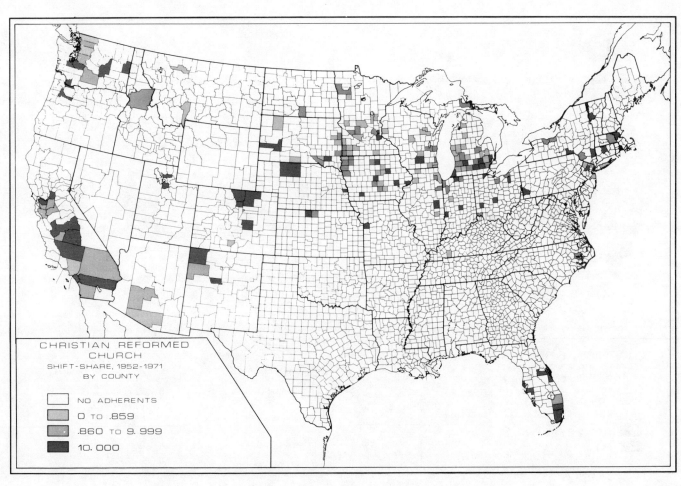

CHRISTIAN REFORMED
CHURCH
SHIFT-SHARE, 1952-1971
BY COUNTY

NO ADHERENTS
0 TO .859
.860 TO 9. 999
10. 000

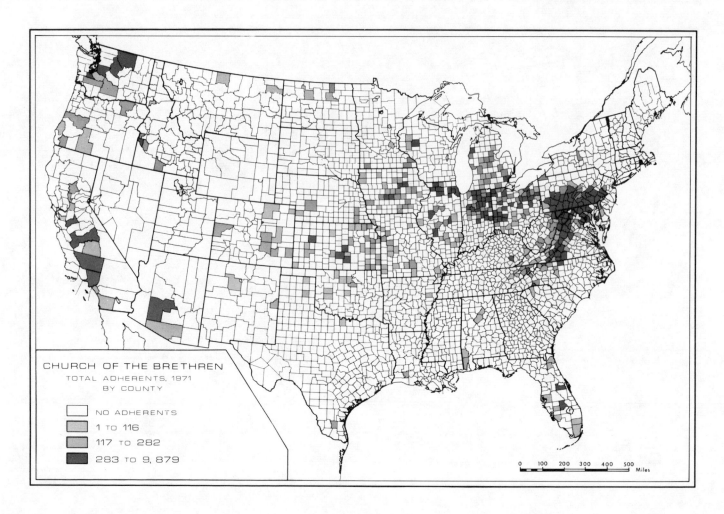

CHURCH OF THE BRETHREN
TOTAL ADHERENTS, 1971
BY COUNTY

NO ADHERENTS
1 TO 116
117 TO 282
283 TO 9,879

0 100 200 300 400 500
Miles

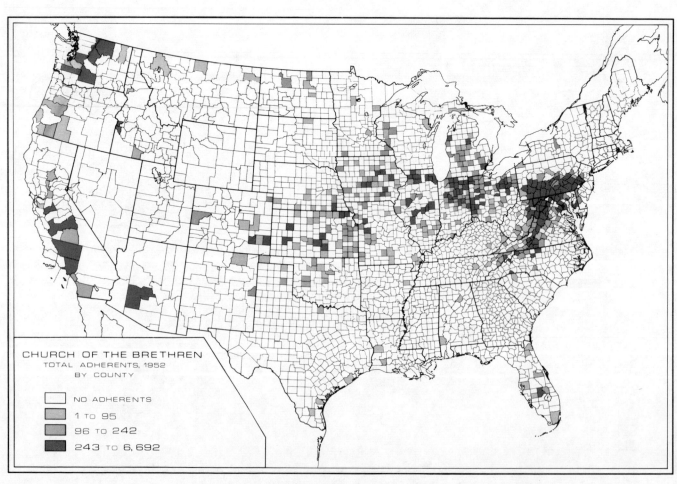

CHURCH OF THE BRETHREN
TOTAL ADHERENTS, 1952
BY COUNTY

NO ADHERENTS
1 TO 95
96 TO 242
243 TO 6,692

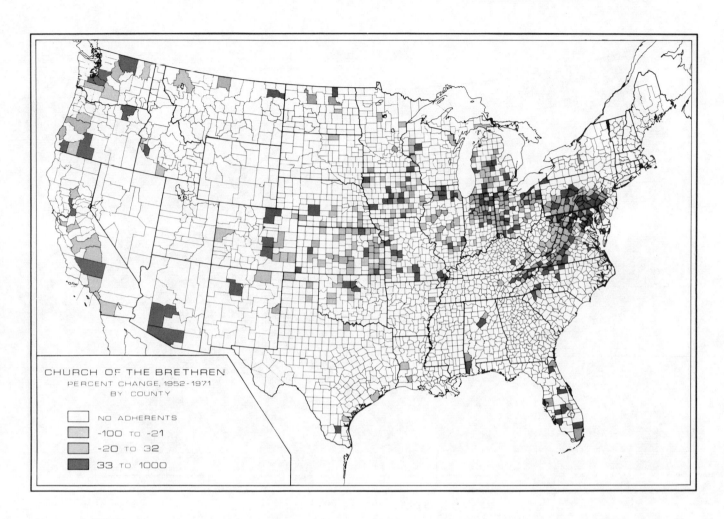

CHURCH OF THE BRETHREN
PERCENT CHANGE, 1952-1971
BY COUNTY

NO ADHERENTS
-100 TO -21
-20 TO 32
33 TO 1000

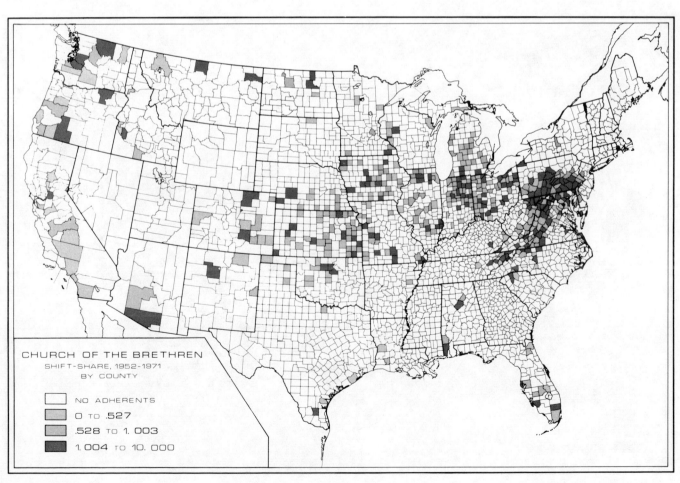

CHURCH OF THE BRETHREN
SHIFT-SHARE, 1952-1971
BY COUNTY

NO ADHERENTS
0 TO .527
.528 TO 1.003
1.004 TO 10.000

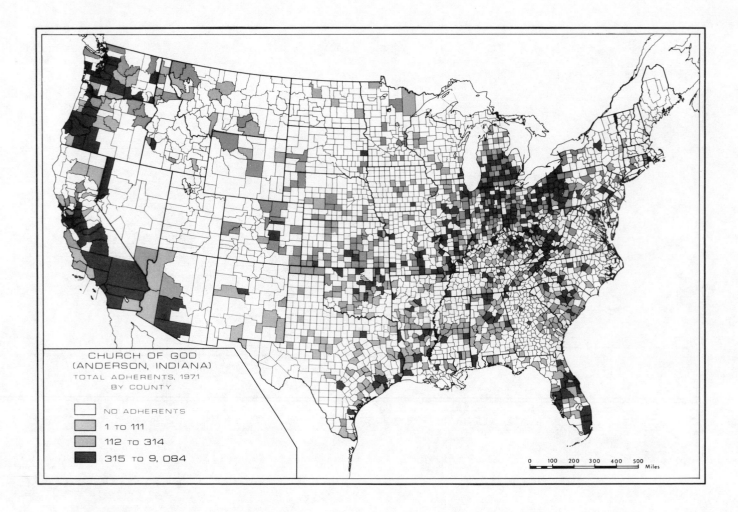

CHURCH OF GOD
(ANDERSON, INDIANA)
TOTAL ADHERENTS, 1971
BY COUNTY

NO ADHERENTS
1 TO 111
112 TO 314
315 TO 9, 084

0   100 200 300 400 500
Miles

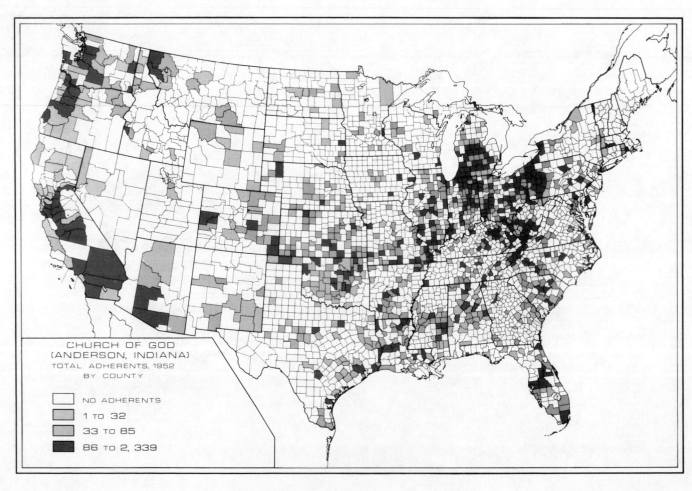

CHURCH OF GOD
(ANDERSON, INDIANA)
TOTAL ADHERENTS, 1952
BY COUNTY

NO ADHERENTS
1 TO 32
33 TO 85
86 TO 2, 339

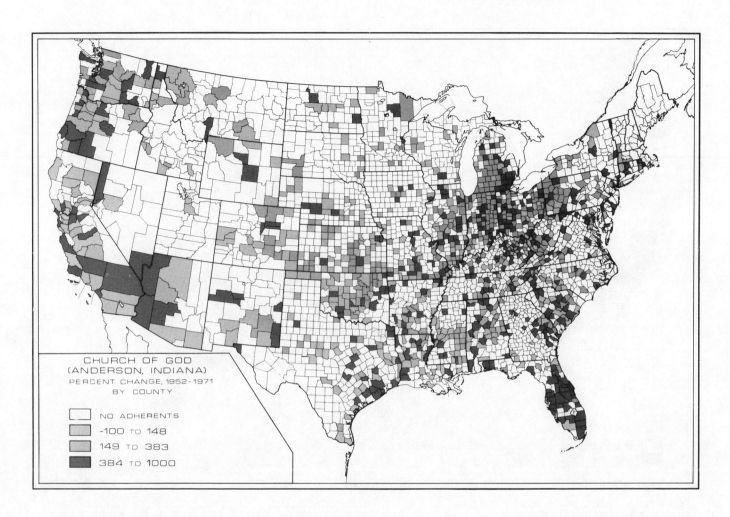

CHURCH OF GOD
(ANDERSON, INDIANA)
PERCENT CHANGE, 1952-1971
BY COUNTY

NO ADHERENTS
-100 TO 148
149 TO 383
384 TO 1000

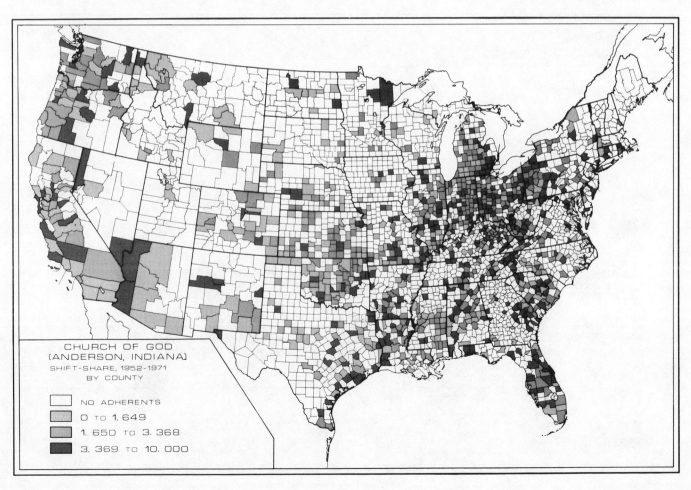

CHURCH OF GOD
(ANDERSON, INDIANA)
SHIFT-SHARE, 1952-1971
BY COUNTY

NO ADHERENTS
0 TO 1.649
1.650 TO 3.368
3.369 TO 10.000

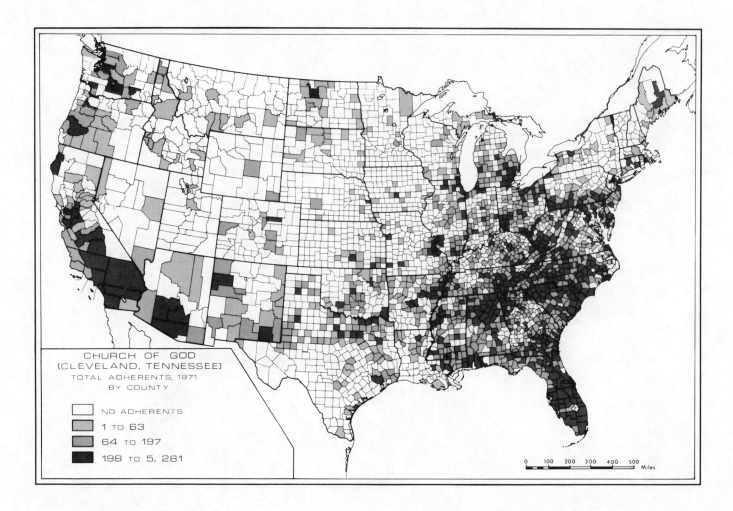

CHURCH OF GOD
(CLEVELAND, TENNESSEE)
TOTAL ADHERENTS, 1971
BY COUNTY

NO ADHERENTS
1 TO 63
64 TO 197
198 TO 5, 281

0   100   200   300   400   500
Miles

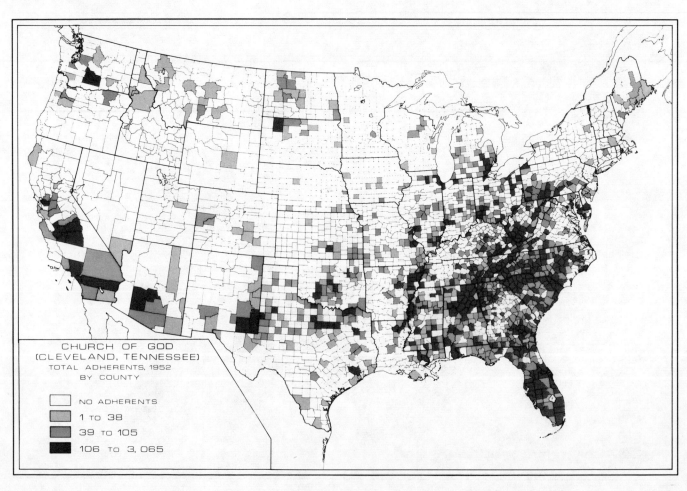

CHURCH OF GOD
(CLEVELAND, TENNESSEE)
TOTAL ADHERENTS, 1952
BY COUNTY

NO ADHERENTS
1 TO 38
39 TO 105
106 TO 3, 065

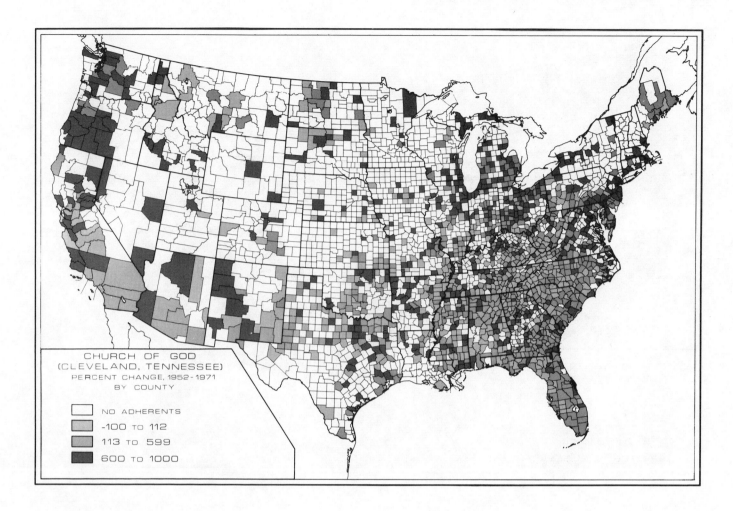

CHURCH OF GOD
(CLEVELAND, TENNESSEE)
PERCENT CHANGE, 1952-1971
BY COUNTY

NO ADHERENTS
-100 TO 112
113 TO 599
600 TO 1000

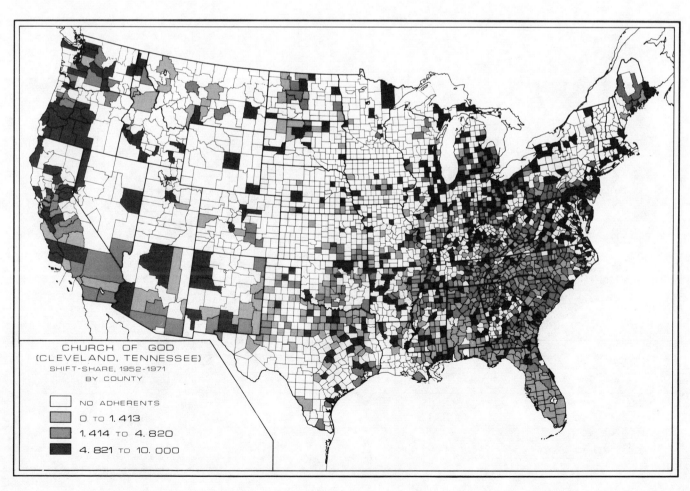

CHURCH OF GOD
(CLEVELAND, TENNESSEE)
SHIFT-SHARE, 1952-1971
BY COUNTY

NO ADHERENTS
0 TO 1.413
1.414 TO 4.820
4.821 TO 10.000

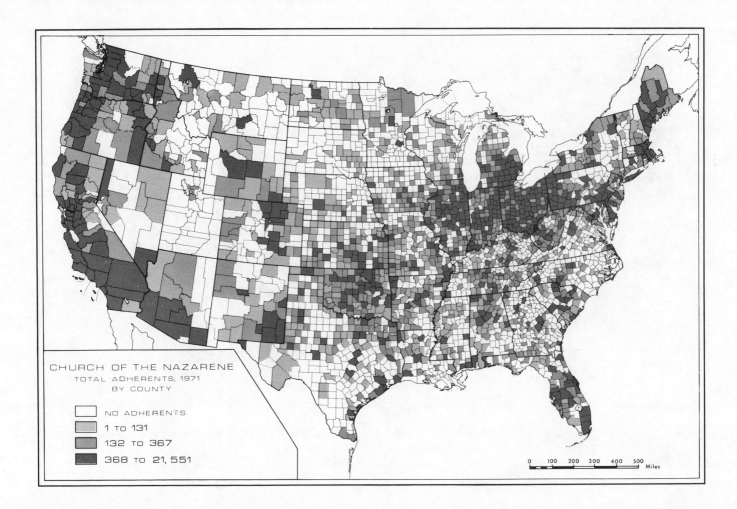

CHURCH OF THE NAZARENE
TOTAL ADHERENTS, 1971
BY COUNTY

- NO ADHERENTS
- 1 TO 131
- 132 TO 367
- 368 TO 21,551

0   100   200   300   400   500
Miles

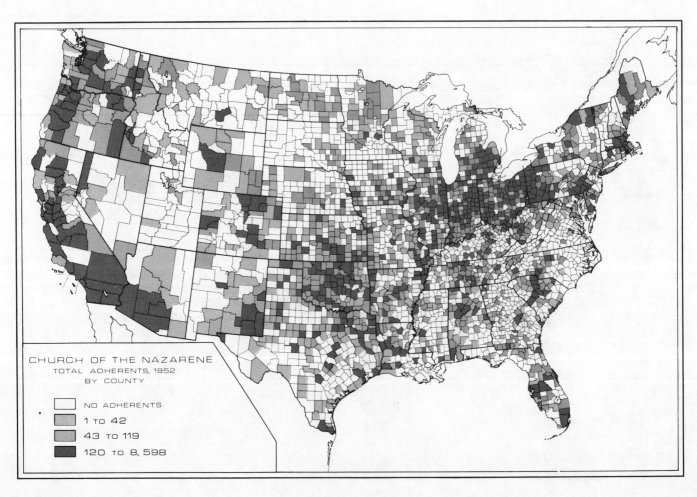

CHURCH OF THE NAZARENE
TOTAL ADHERENTS, 1952
BY COUNTY

- NO ADHERENTS
- 1 TO 42
- 43 TO 119
- 120 TO 8,598

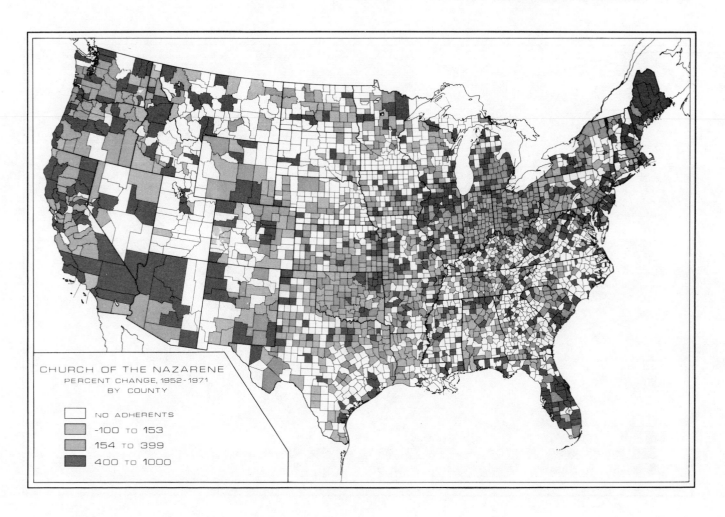

CHURCH OF THE NAZARENE
PERCENT CHANGE, 1952-1971
BY COUNTY

- NO ADHERENTS
- -100 TO 153
- 154 TO 399
- 400 TO 1000

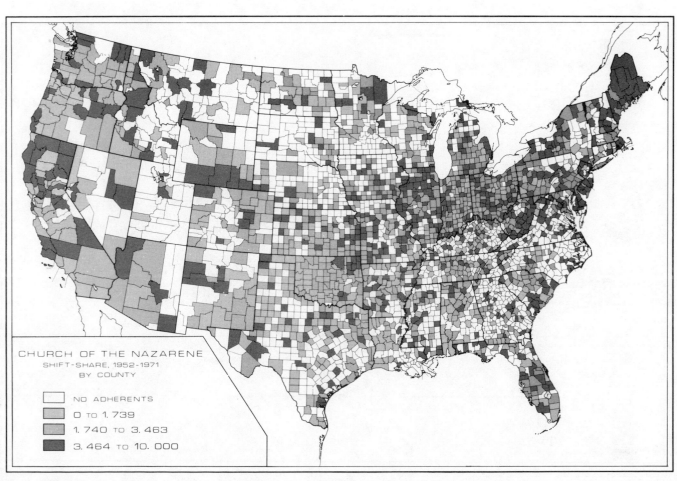

CHURCH OF THE NAZARENE
SHIFT-SHARE, 1952-1971
BY COUNTY

- NO ADHERENTS
- 0 TO 1. 739
- 1. 740 TO 3. 463
- 3. 464 TO 10. 000

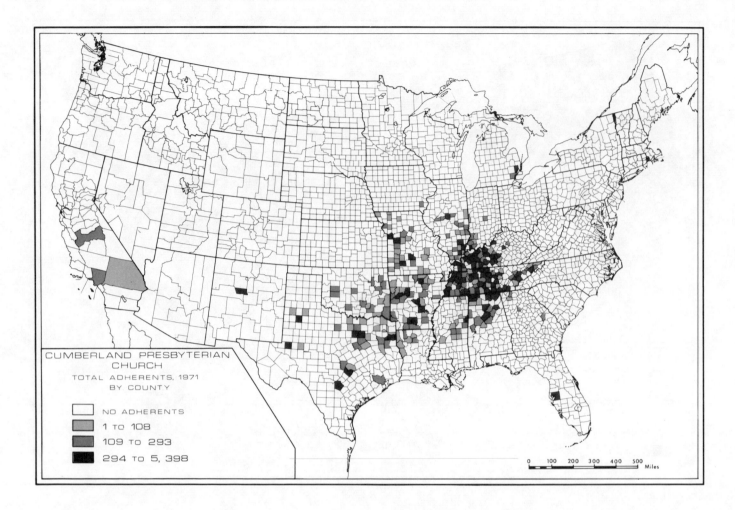

CUMBERLAND PRESBYTERIAN
CHURCH
TOTAL ADHERENTS, 1971
BY COUNTY

NO ADHERENTS
1 TO 108
109 TO 293
294 TO 5, 398

0   100   200   300   400   500
Miles

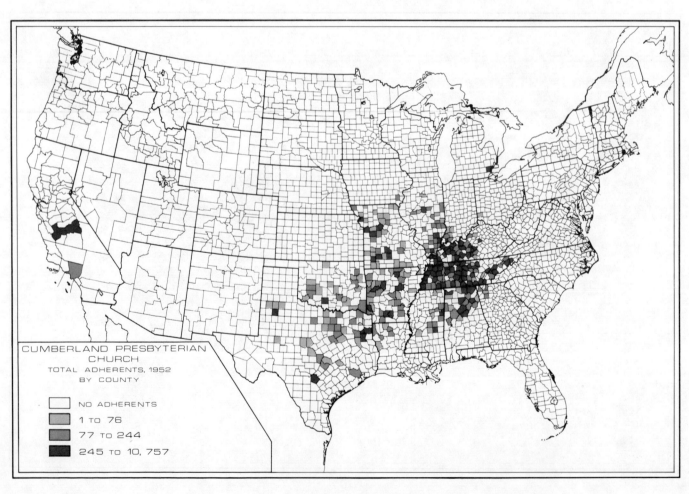

CUMBERLAND PRESBYTERIAN
CHURCH
TOTAL ADHERENTS, 1952
BY COUNTY

NO ADHERENTS
1 TO 76
77 TO 244
245 TO 10, 757

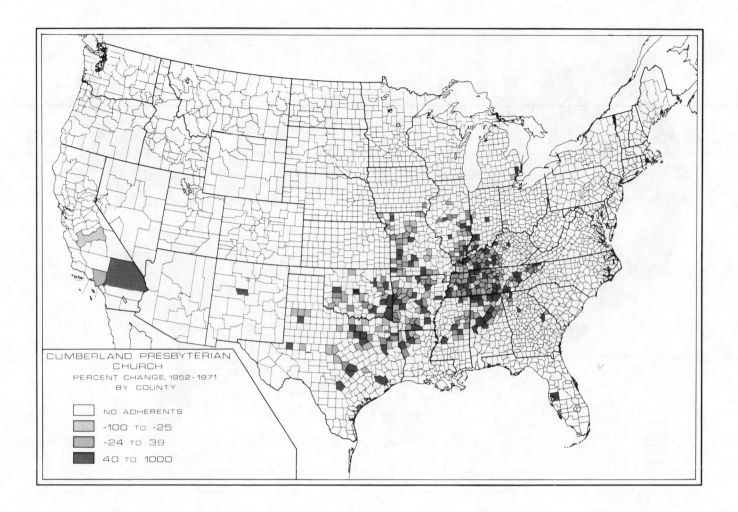

CUMBERLAND PRESBYTERIAN
CHURCH
PERCENT CHANGE, 1952-1971
BY COUNTY

    NO ADHERENTS
    -100 TO -25
    -24 TO 39
    40 TO 1000

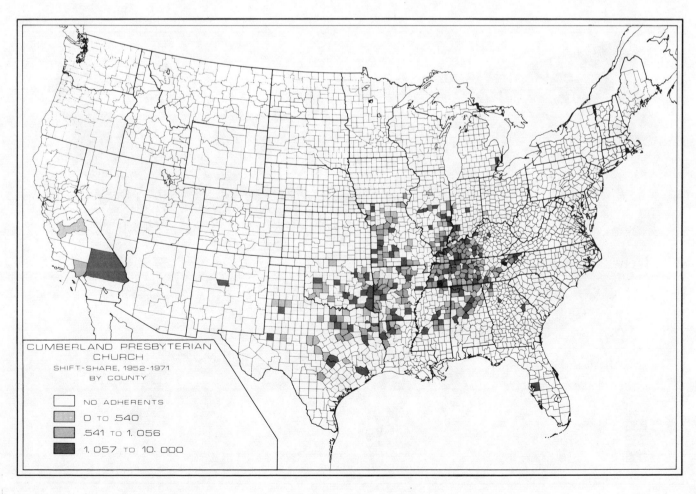

CUMBERLAND PRESBYTERIAN
CHURCH
SHIFT-SHARE, 1952-1971
BY COUNTY

    NO ADHERENTS
    0 TO .540
    .541 TO 1.056
    1.057 TO 10.000

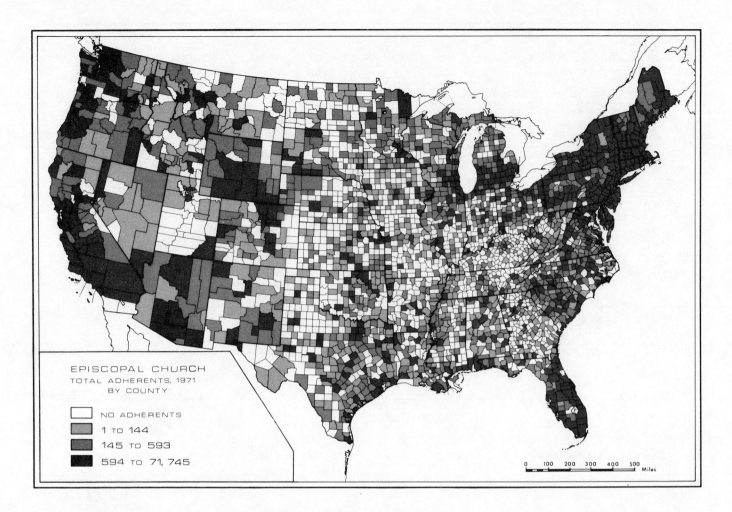

EPISCOPAL CHURCH
TOTAL ADHERENTS, 1971
BY COUNTY

☐ NO ADHERENTS
▨ 1 TO 144
▨ 145 TO 593
■ 594 TO 71,745

0 100 200 300 400 500 Miles

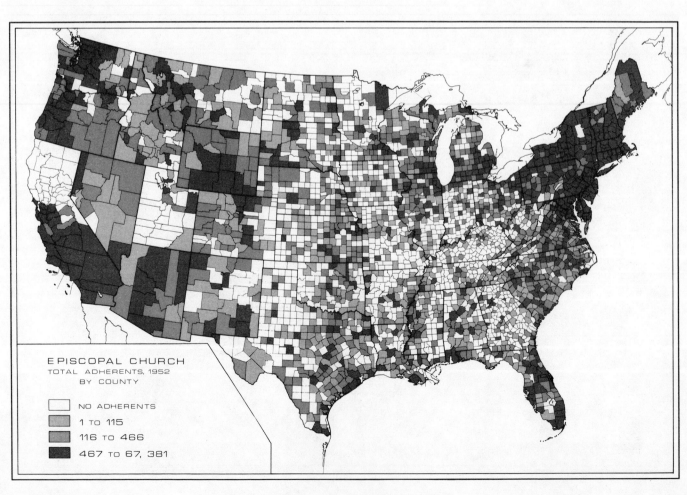

EPISCOPAL CHURCH
TOTAL ADHERENTS, 1952
BY COUNTY

☐ NO ADHERENTS
▨ 1 TO 115
▨ 116 TO 466
■ 467 TO 67,381

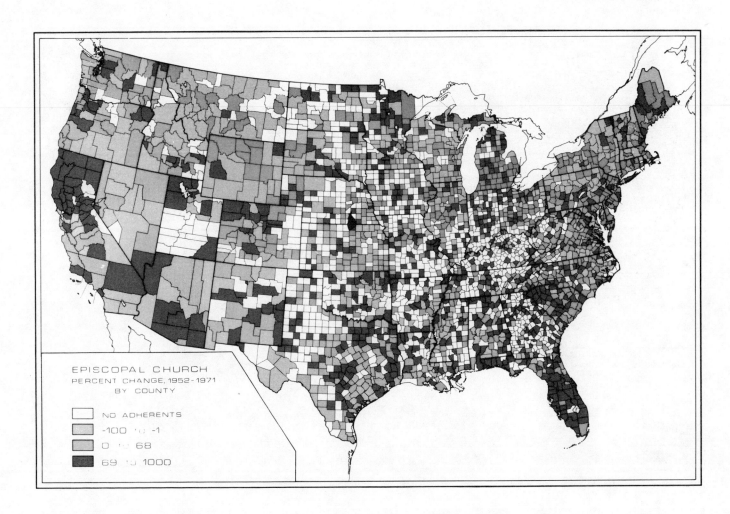

EPISCOPAL CHURCH
PERCENT CHANGE, 1952-1971
BY COUNTY

☐ NO ADHERENTS
▨ -100 to -1
▨ 0 to 68
■ 69 to 1000

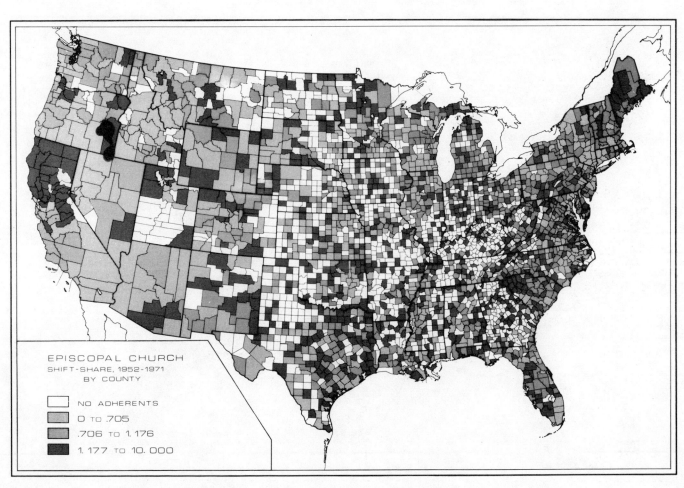

EPISCOPAL CHURCH
SHIFT-SHARE, 1952-1971
BY COUNTY

☐ NO ADHERENTS
▨ 0 to .705
▨ .706 to 1.176
■ 1.177 to 10.000

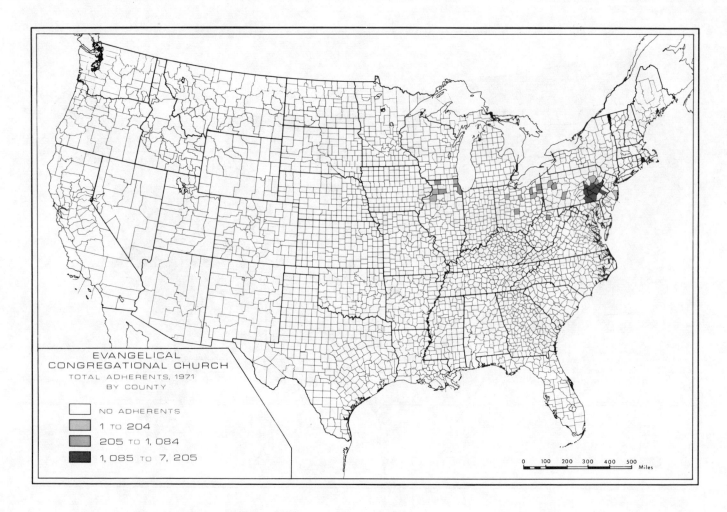

EVANGELICAL
CONGREGATIONAL CHURCH
TOTAL ADHERENTS, 1971
BY COUNTY

NO ADHERENTS
1 TO 204
205 TO 1,084
1,085 TO 7,205

0   100 200 300 400 500
Miles

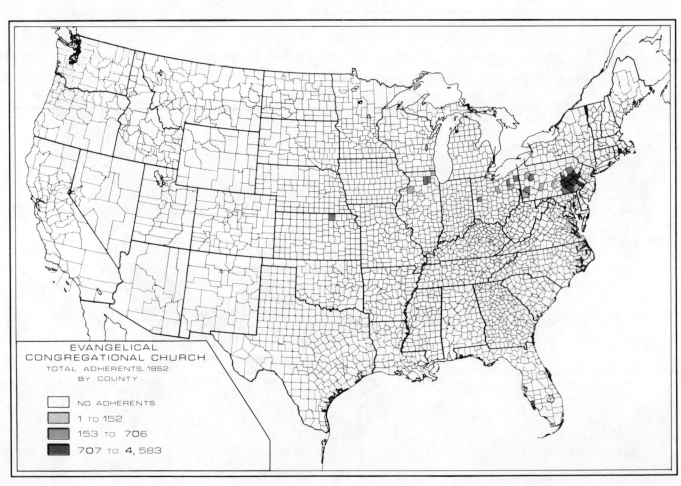

EVANGELICAL
CONGREGATIONAL CHURCH
TOTAL ADHERENTS, 1952
BY COUNTY

NO ADHERENTS
1 TO 152
153 TO 706
707 TO 4,583

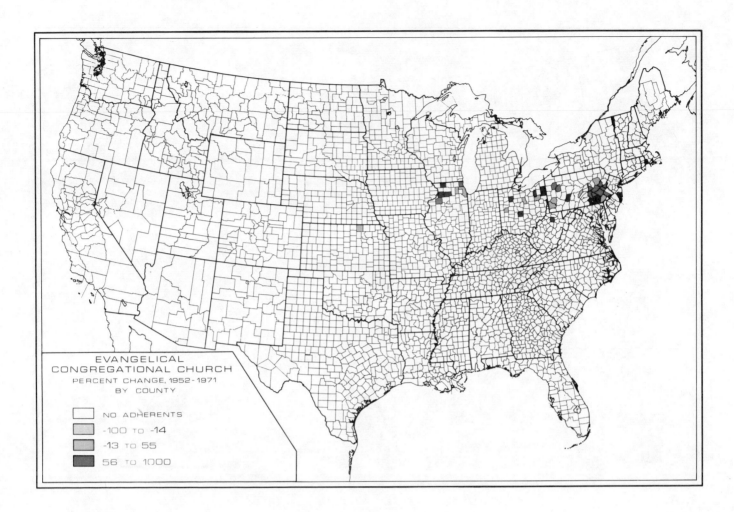

EVANGELICAL
CONGREGATIONAL CHURCH
PERCENT CHANGE, 1952-1971
BY COUNTY

- NO ADHERENTS
- -100 TO -14
- -13 TO 55
- 56 TO 1000

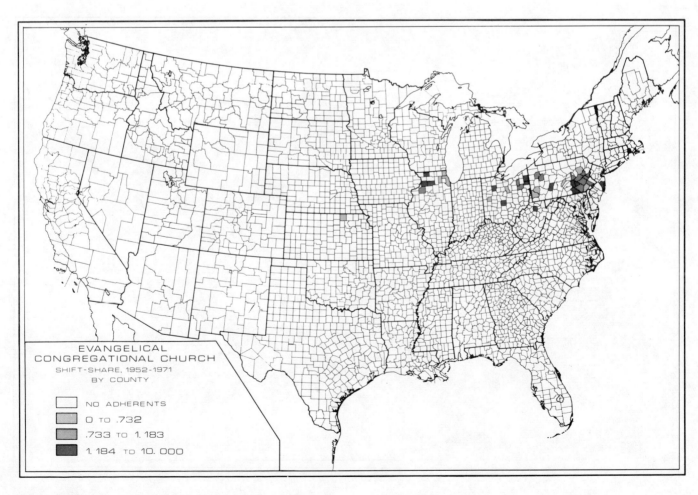

EVANGELICAL
CONGREGATIONAL CHURCH
SHIFT-SHARE, 1952-1971
BY COUNTY

- NO ADHERENTS
- 0 TO .732
- .733 TO 1.183
- 1.184 TO 10.000

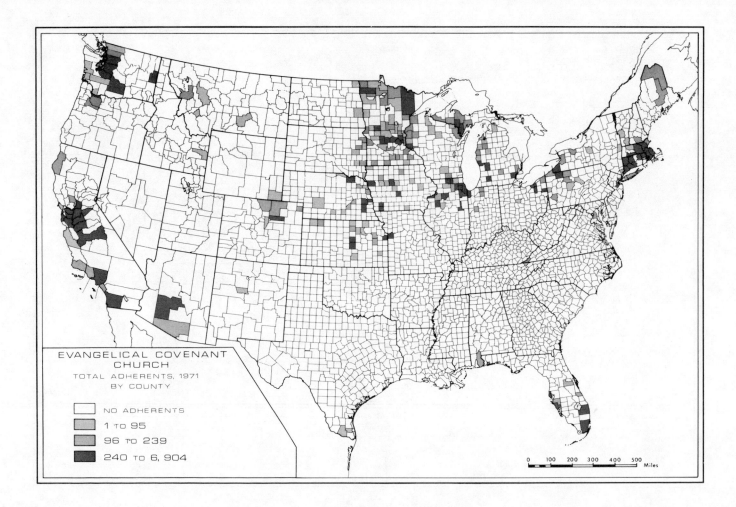

EVANGELICAL COVENANT
CHURCH
TOTAL ADHERENTS, 1971
BY COUNTY

NO ADHERENTS
1 TO 95
96 TO 239
240 TO 6, 904

0   100   200   300   400   500
                              Miles

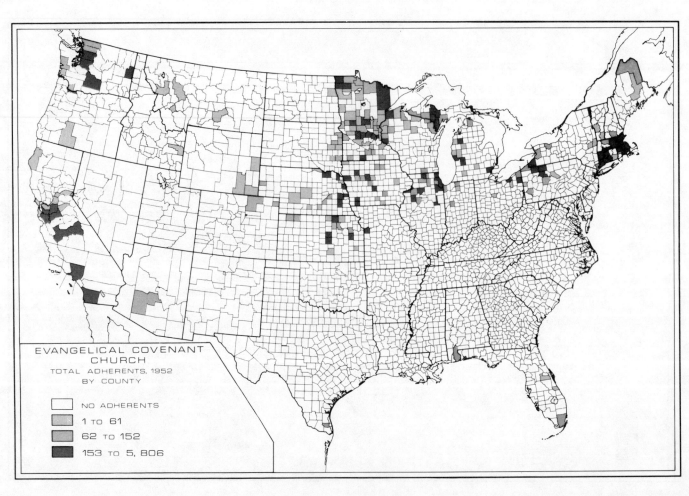

EVANGELICAL COVENANT
CHURCH
TOTAL ADHERENTS, 1952
BY COUNTY

NO ADHERENTS
1 TO 61
62 TO 152
153 TO 5, 806

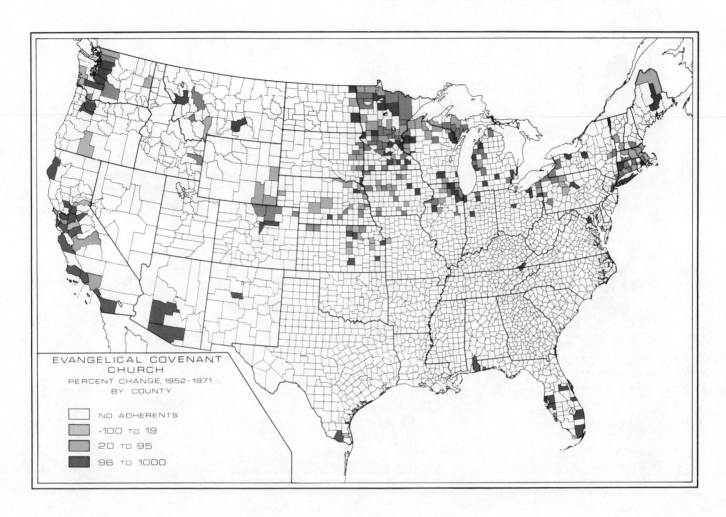

EVANGELICAL COVENANT
CHURCH
PERCENT CHANGE, 1952-1971
BY COUNTY

NO ADHERENTS
-100 TO 19
20 TO 95
96 TO 1000

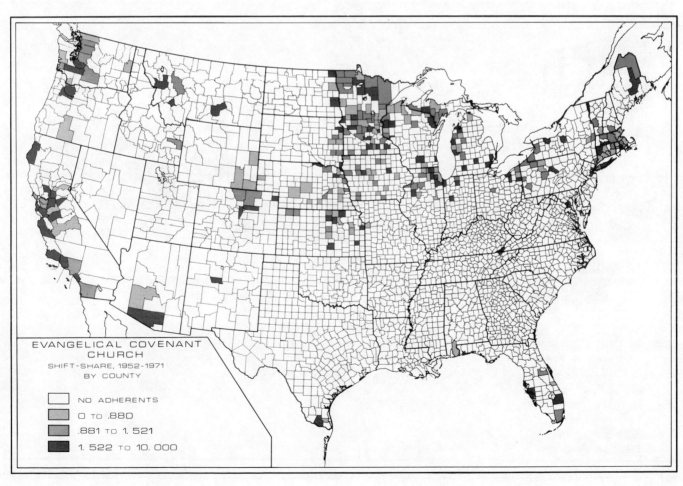

EVANGELICAL COVENANT
CHURCH
SHIFT-SHARE, 1952-1971
BY COUNTY

NO ADHERENTS
0 TO .880
.881 TO 1. 521
1. 522 TO 10. 000

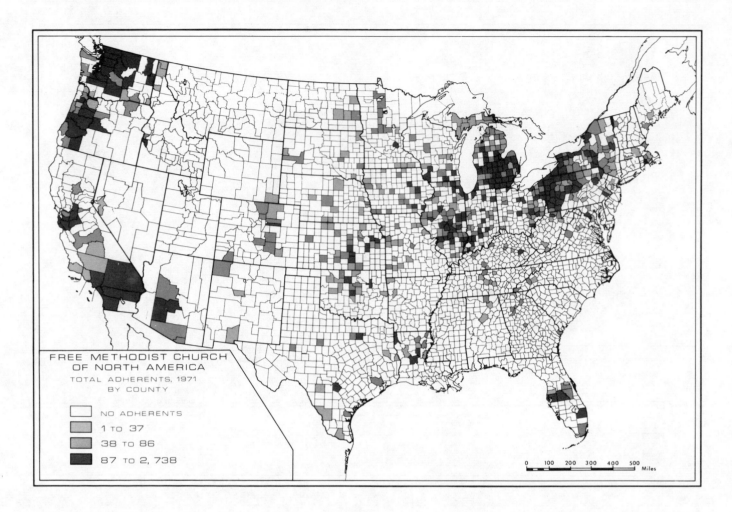

FREE METHODIST CHURCH
OF NORTH AMERICA
TOTAL ADHERENTS, 1971
BY COUNTY

NO ADHERENTS
1 TO 37
38 TO 86
87 TO 2, 738

0   100   200   300   400   500
Miles

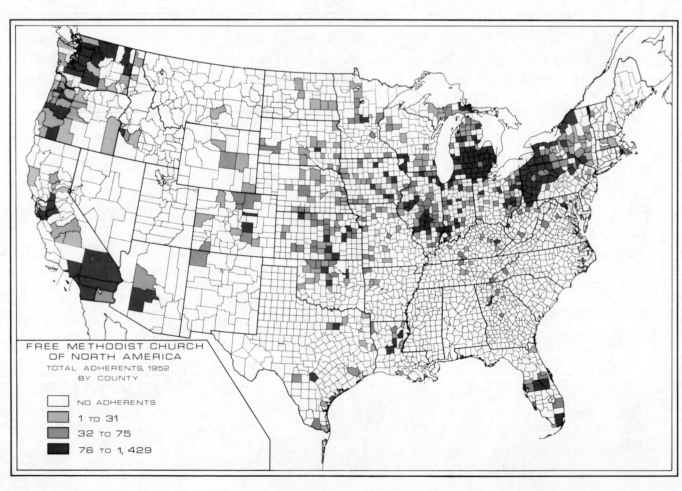

FREE METHODIST CHURCH
OF NORTH AMERICA
TOTAL ADHERENTS, 1952
BY COUNTY

NO ADHERENTS
1 TO 31
32 TO 75
76 TO 1, 429

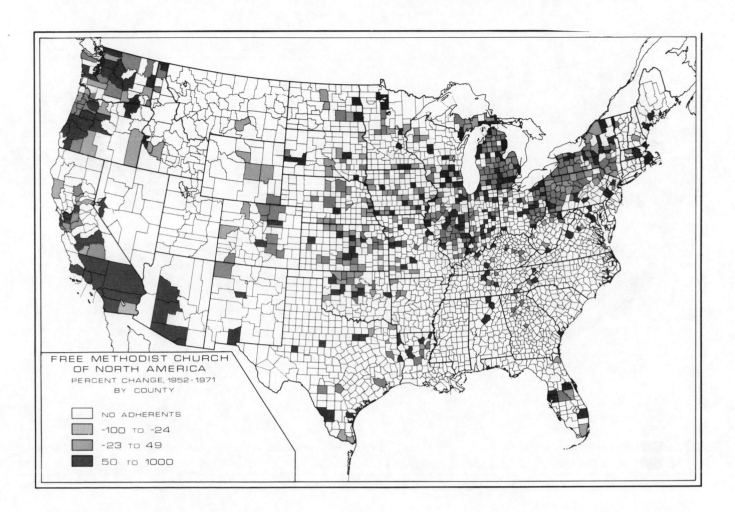

FREE METHODIST CHURCH
OF NORTH AMERICA
PERCENT CHANGE, 1952-1971
BY COUNTY

- NO ADHERENTS
- -100 TO -24
- -23 TO 49
- 50 TO 1000

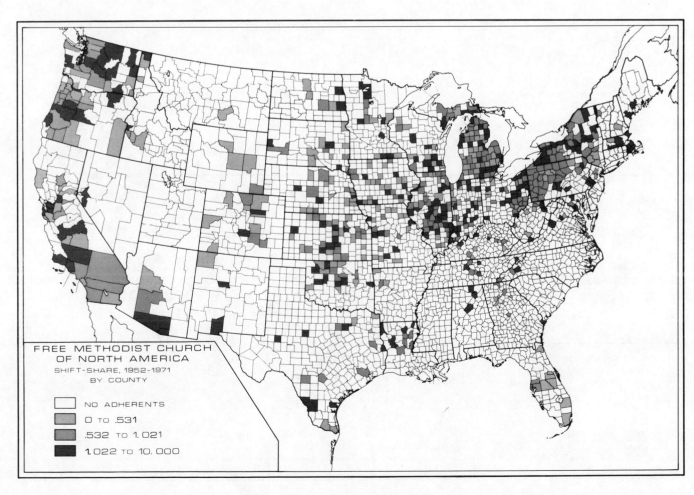

FREE METHODIST CHURCH
OF NORTH AMERICA
SHIFT-SHARE, 1952-1971
BY COUNTY

- NO ADHERENTS
- 0 TO .531
- .532 TO 1.021
- 1.022 TO 10.000

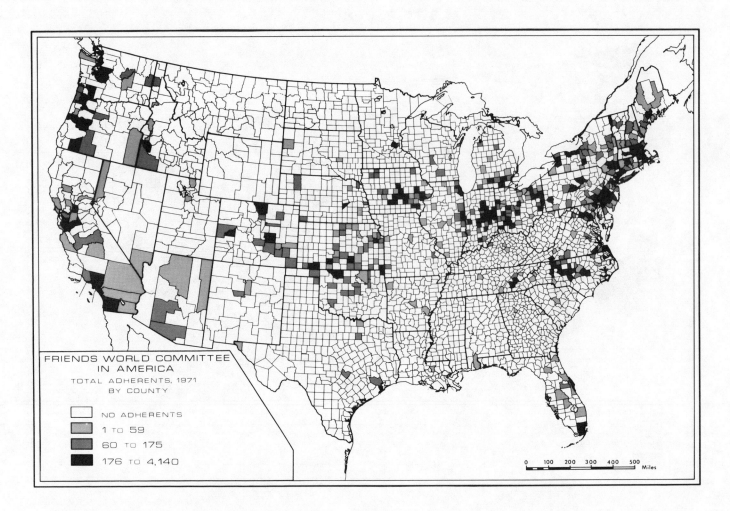

FRIENDS WORLD COMMITTEE
IN AMERICA
TOTAL ADHERENTS, 1971
BY COUNTY

NO ADHERENTS
1 TO 59
60 TO 175
176 TO 4,140

0 100 200 300 400 500
Miles

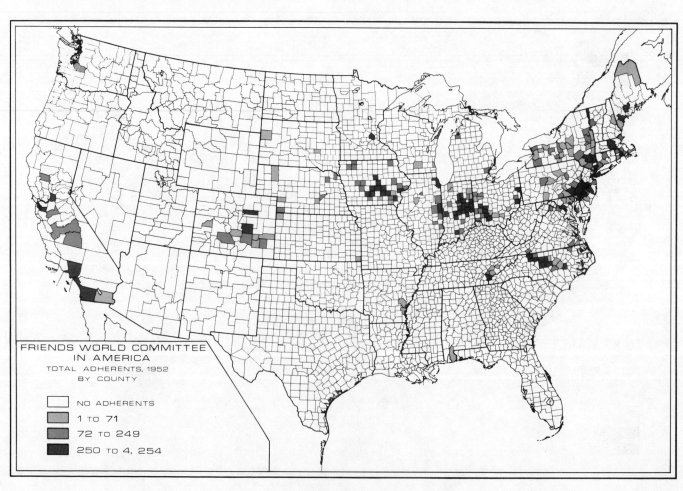

FRIENDS WORLD COMMITTEE
IN AMERICA
TOTAL ADHERENTS, 1952
BY COUNTY

NO ADHERENTS
1 TO 71
72 TO 249
250 TO 4, 254

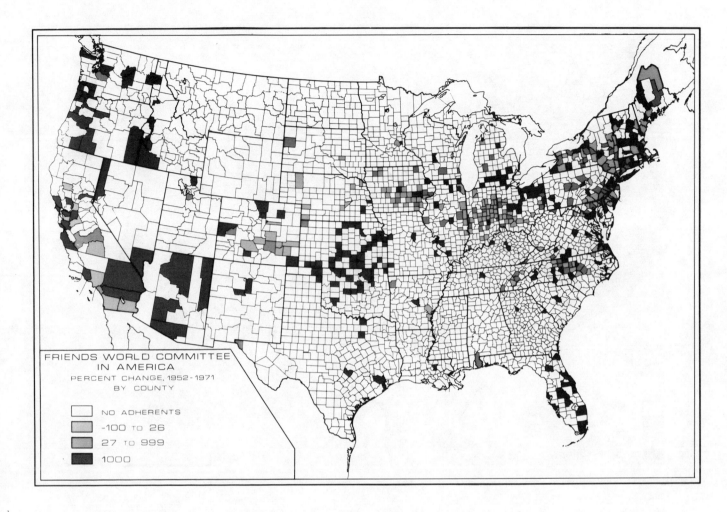

FRIENDS WORLD COMMITTEE
IN AMERICA
PERCENT CHANGE, 1952-1971
BY COUNTY

NO ADHERENTS
-100 TO 26
27 TO 999
1000

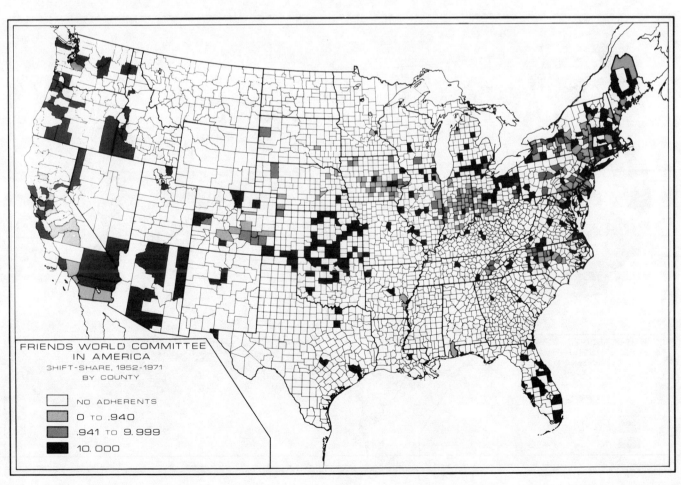

FRIENDS WORLD COMMITTEE
IN AMERICA
SHIFT-SHARE, 1952-1971
BY COUNTY

NO ADHERENTS
0 TO .940
.941 TO 9.999
10.000

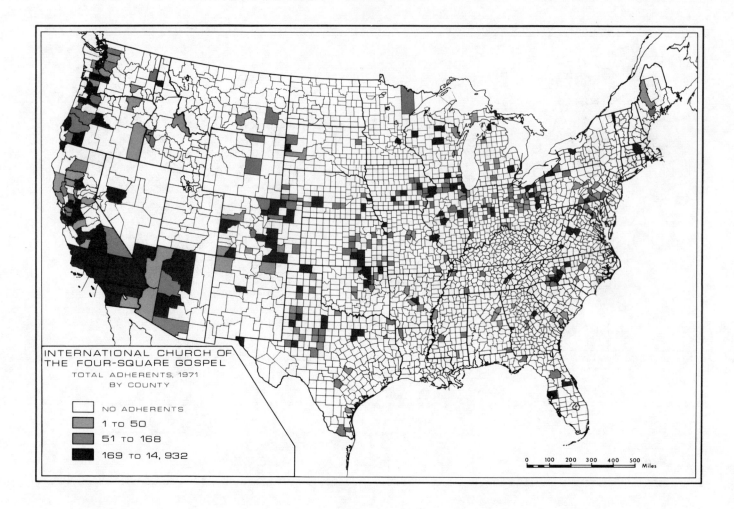

INTERNATIONAL CHURCH OF
THE FOUR-SQUARE GOSPEL

TOTAL ADHERENTS, 1971
BY COUNTY

NO ADHERENTS
1 TO 50
51 TO 168
169 TO 14,932

0   100   200   300   400   500
Miles

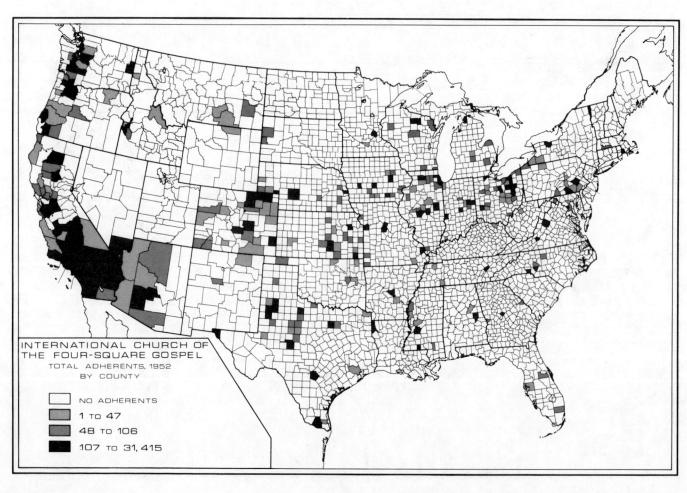

INTERNATIONAL CHURCH OF
THE FOUR-SQUARE GOSPEL

TOTAL ADHERENTS, 1952
BY COUNTY

NO ADHERENTS
1 TO 47
48 TO 106
107 TO 31,415

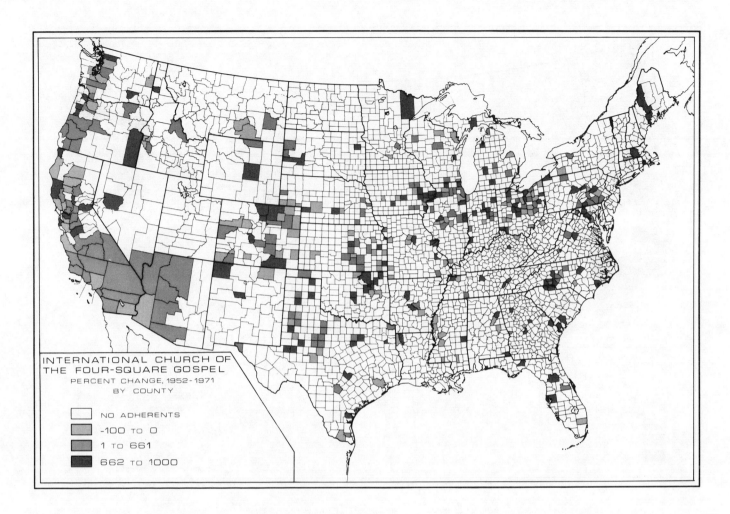

INTERNATIONAL CHURCH OF
THE FOUR-SQUARE GOSPEL
PERCENT CHANGE, 1952-1971
BY COUNTY

- NO ADHERENTS
- -100 TO 0
- 1 TO 661
- 662 TO 1000

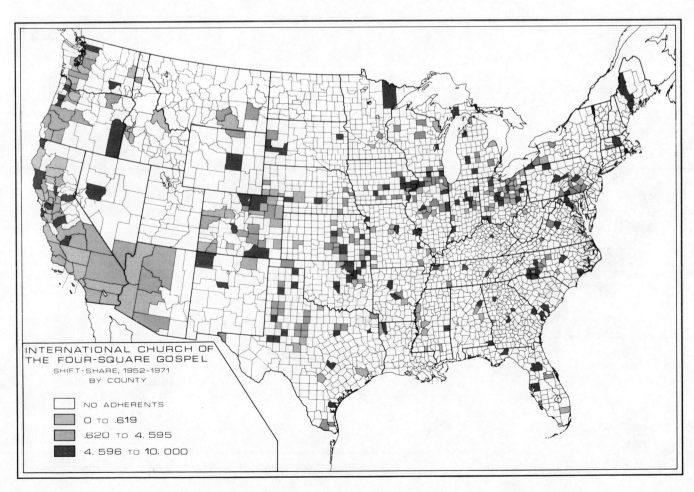

INTERNATIONAL CHURCH OF
THE FOUR-SQUARE GOSPEL
SHIFT-SHARE, 1952-1971
BY COUNTY

- NO ADHERENTS
- 0 TO .619
- .620 TO 4.595
- 4.596 TO 10.000

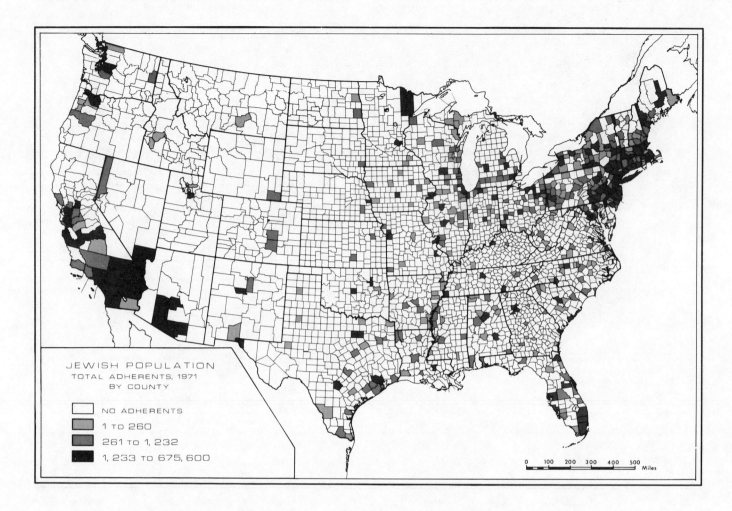

JEWISH POPULATION
TOTAL ADHERENTS, 1971
BY COUNTY

☐ NO ADHERENTS
▨ 1 TO 260
▨ 261 TO 1,232
■ 1,233 TO 675,600

0　100　200　300　400　500
Miles

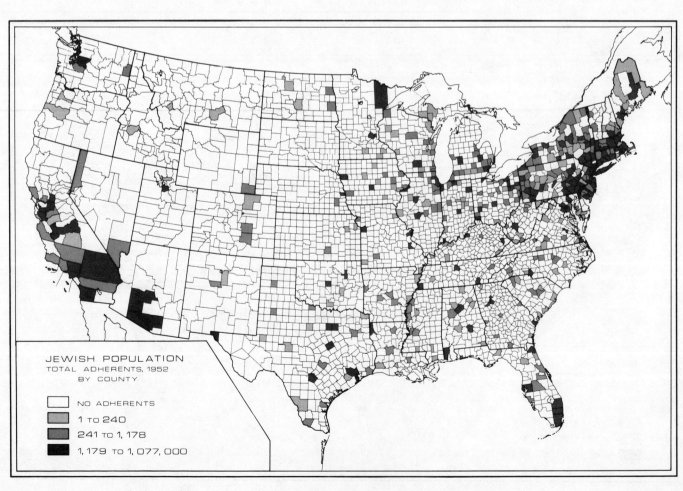

JEWISH POPULATION
TOTAL ADHERENTS, 1952
BY COUNTY

☐ NO ADHERENTS
▨ 1 TO 240
▨ 241 TO 1,178
■ 1,179 TO 1,077,000

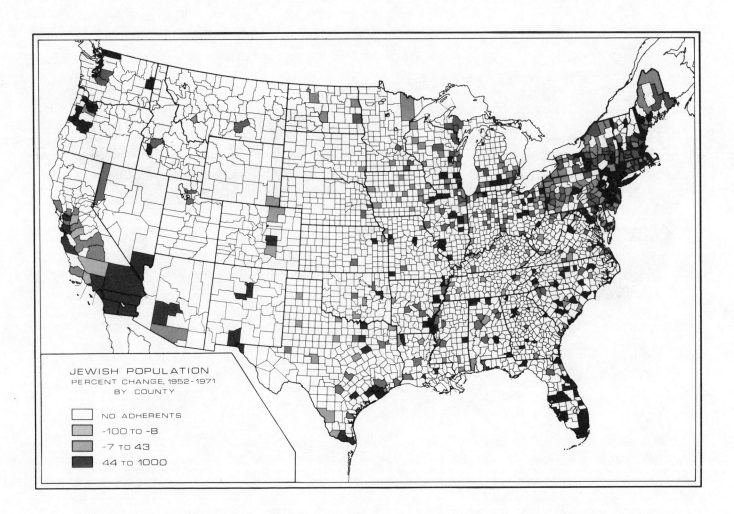

JEWISH POPULATION
PERCENT CHANGE, 1952-1971
BY COUNTY

NO ADHERENTS
-100 TO -8
-7 TO 43
44 TO 1000

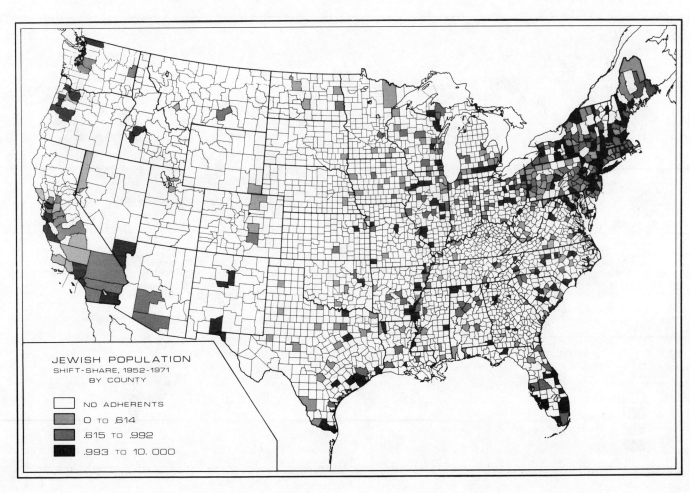

JEWISH POPULATION
SHIFT-SHARE, 1952-1971
BY COUNTY

NO ADHERENTS
0 TO .614
.615 TO .992
.993 TO 10.000

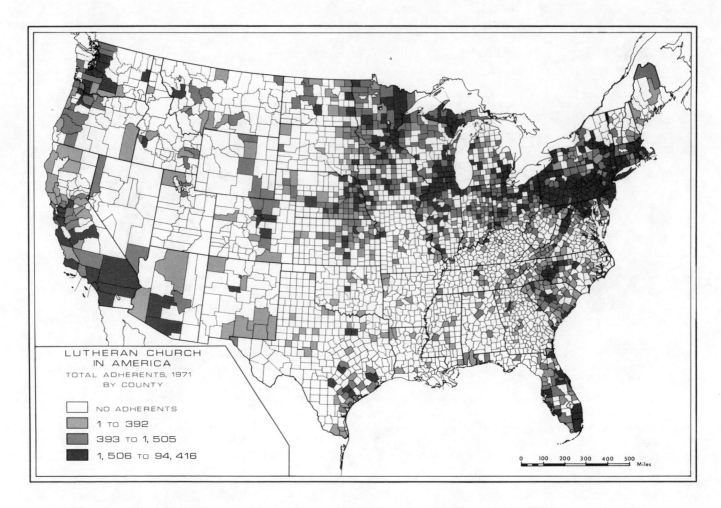

LUTHERAN CHURCH
IN AMERICA
TOTAL ADHERENTS, 1971
BY COUNTY

NO ADHERENTS
1 TO 392
393 TO 1,505
1,506 TO 94,416

0   100   200   300   400   500
Miles

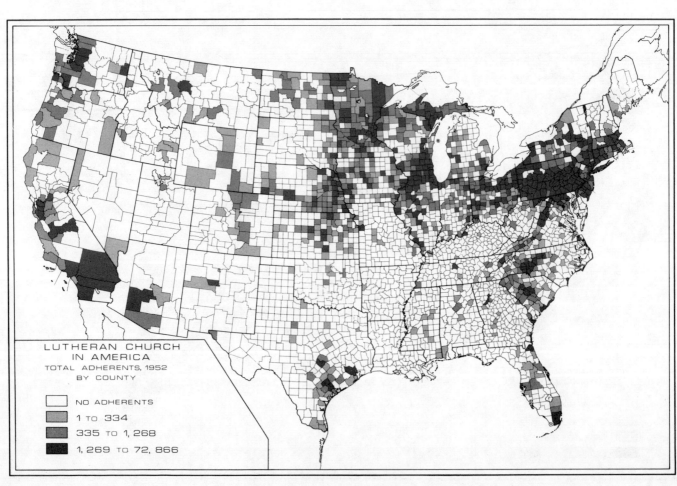

LUTHERAN CHURCH
IN AMERICA
TOTAL ADHERENTS, 1952
BY COUNTY

NO ADHERENTS
1 TO 334
335 TO 1,268
1,269 TO 72,866

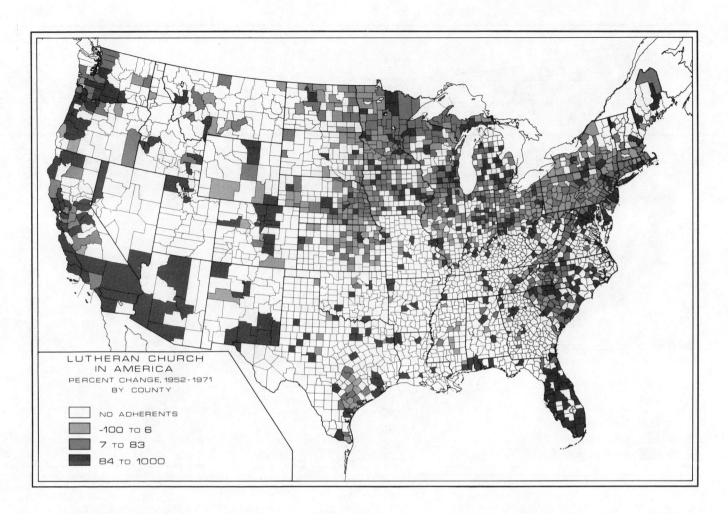

LUTHERAN CHURCH
IN AMERICA
PERCENT CHANGE, 1952-1971
BY COUNTY

NO ADHERENTS
-100 TO 6
7 TO 83
84 TO 1000

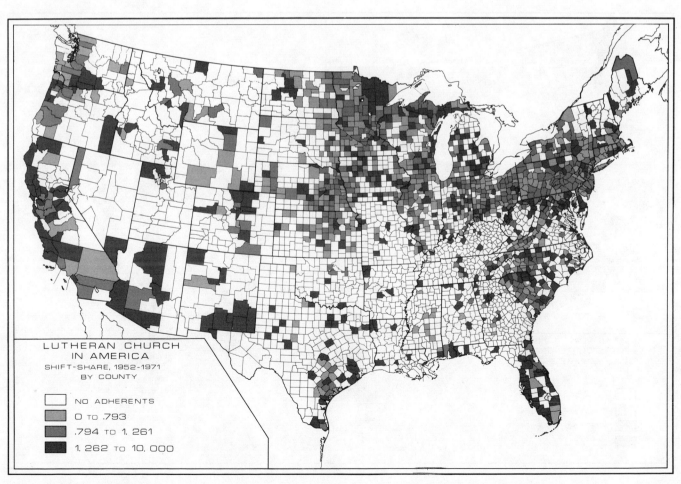

LUTHERAN CHURCH
IN AMERICA
SHIFT-SHARE, 1952-1971
BY COUNTY

NO ADHERENTS
0 TO .793
.794 TO 1. 261
1. 262 TO 10. 000

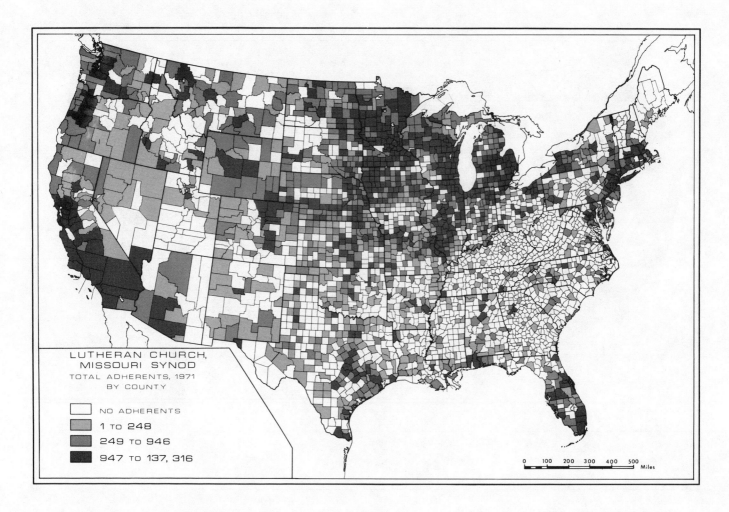

LUTHERAN CHURCH,
MISSOURI SYNOD
TOTAL ADHERENTS, 1971
BY COUNTY

NO ADHERENTS
1 TO 248
249 TO 946
947 TO 137, 316

0   100   200   300   400   500
Miles

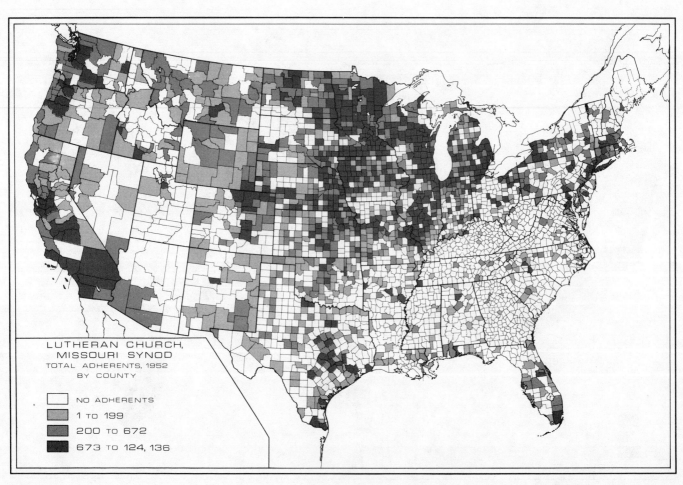

LUTHERAN CHURCH,
MISSOURI SYNOD
TOTAL ADHERENTS, 1952
BY COUNTY

NO ADHERENTS
1 TO 199
200 TO 672
673 TO 124, 136

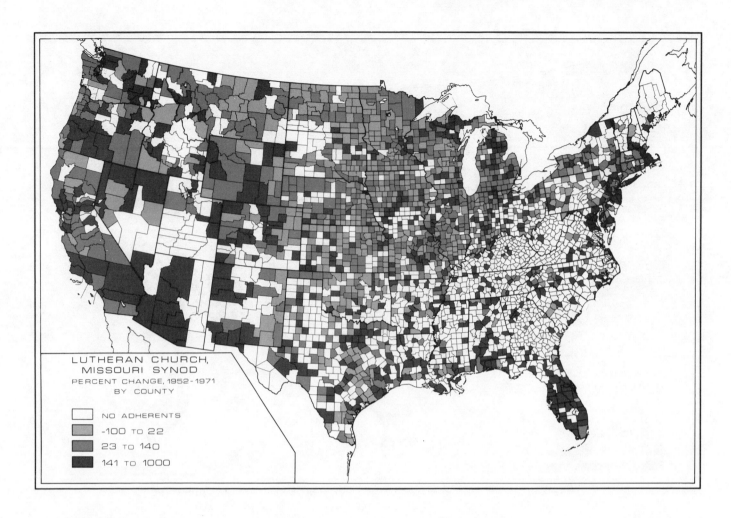

LUTHERAN CHURCH,
MISSOURI SYNOD
PERCENT CHANGE, 1952-1971
BY COUNTY

NO ADHERENTS
-100 TO 22
23 TO 140
141 TO 1000

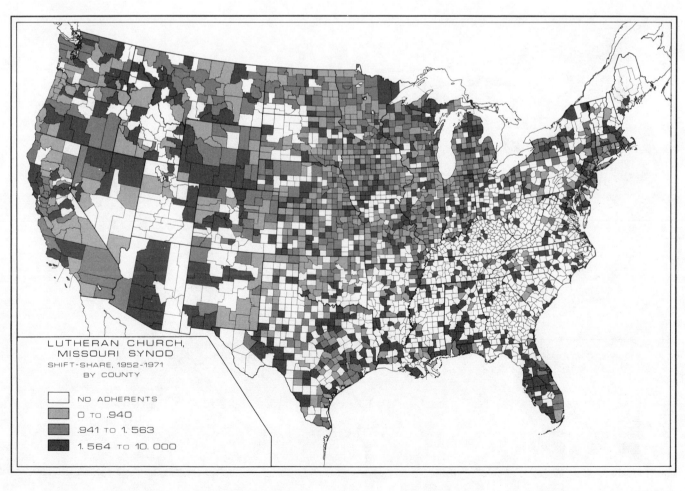

LUTHERAN CHURCH,
MISSOURI SYNOD
SHIFT-SHARE, 1952-1971
BY COUNTY

NO ADHERENTS
0 TO .940
.941 TO 1. 563
1. 564 TO 10. 000

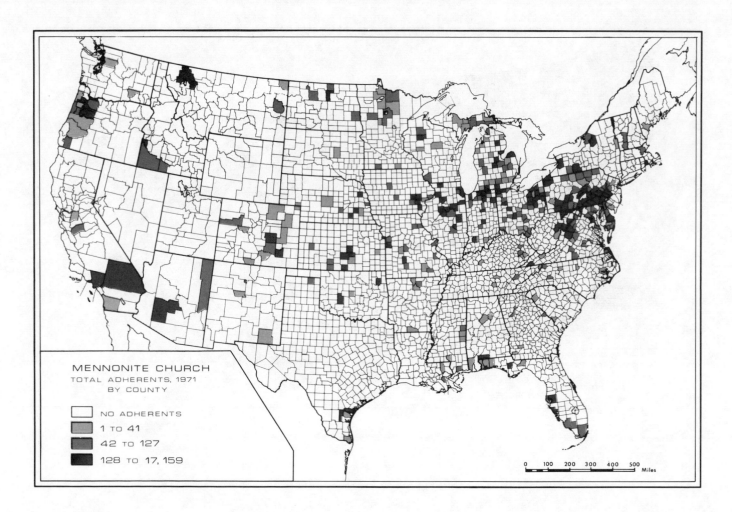

MENNONITE CHURCH
TOTAL ADHERENTS, 1971
BY COUNTY

NO ADHERENTS
1 TO 41
42 TO 127
128 TO 17, 159

0 100 200 300 400 500
Miles

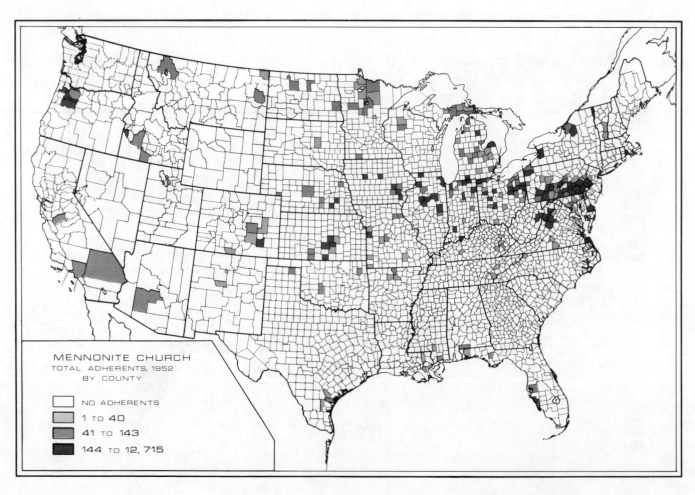

MENNONITE CHURCH
TOTAL ADHERENTS, 1952
BY COUNTY

NO ADHERENTS
1 TO 40
41 TO 143
144 TO 12, 715

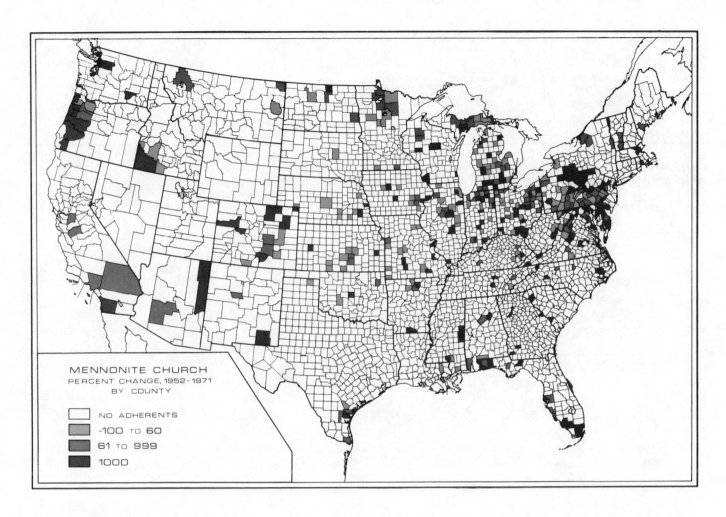

MENNONITE CHURCH
PERCENT CHANGE, 1952-1971
BY COUNTY

NO ADHERENTS
-100 TO 60
61 TO 999
1000

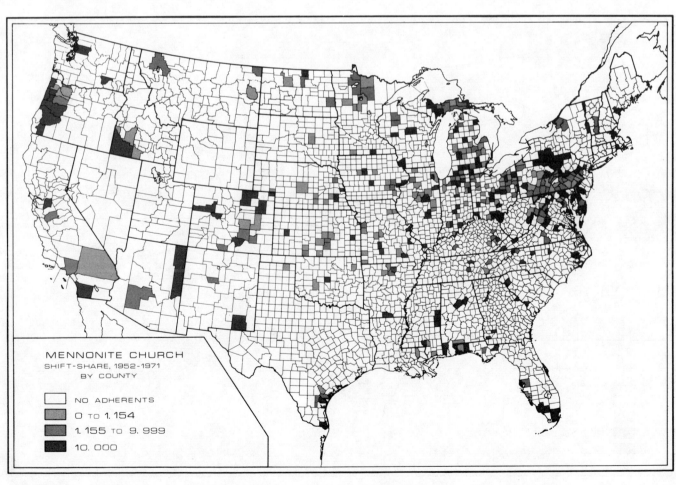

MENNONITE CHURCH
SHIFT-SHARE, 1952-1971
BY COUNTY

NO ADHERENTS
0 TO 1.154
1.155 TO 9.999
10.000

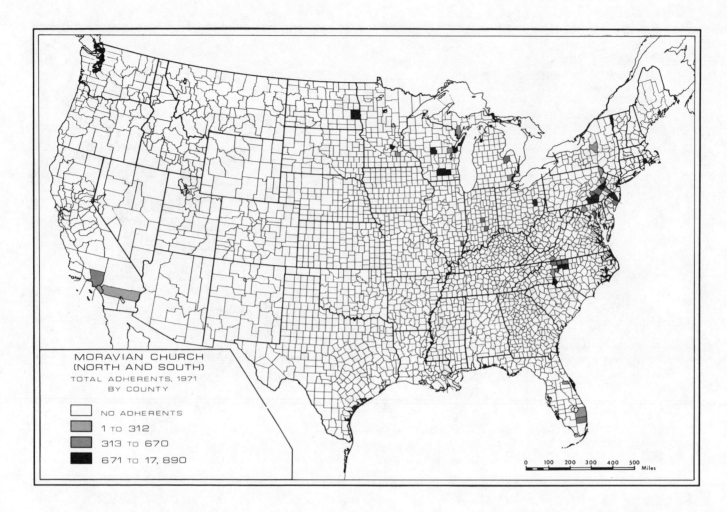

MORAVIAN CHURCH
(NORTH AND SOUTH)
TOTAL ADHERENTS, 1971
BY COUNTY

NO ADHERENTS
1 TO 312
313 TO 670
671 TO 17,890

0   100   200   300   400   500
Miles

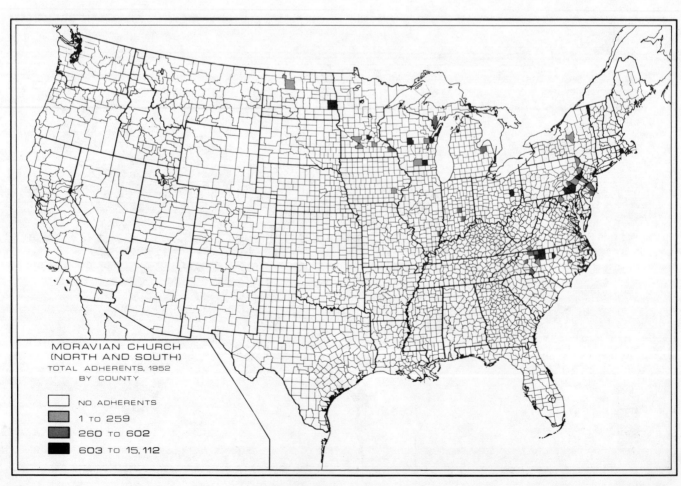

MORAVIAN CHURCH
(NORTH AND SOUTH)
TOTAL ADHERENTS, 1952
BY COUNTY

NO ADHERENTS
1 TO 259
260 TO 602
603 TO 15,112

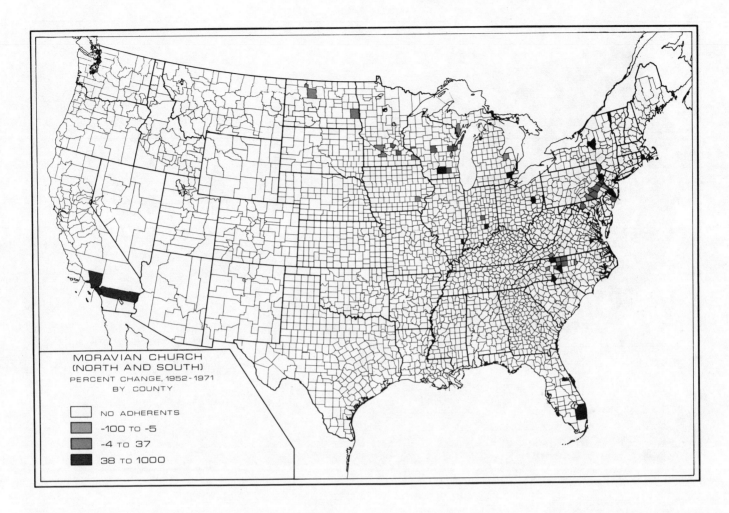

MORAVIAN CHURCH
(NORTH AND SOUTH)
PERCENT CHANGE, 1952-1971
BY COUNTY

NO ADHERENTS
-100 TO -5
-4 TO 37
38 TO 1000

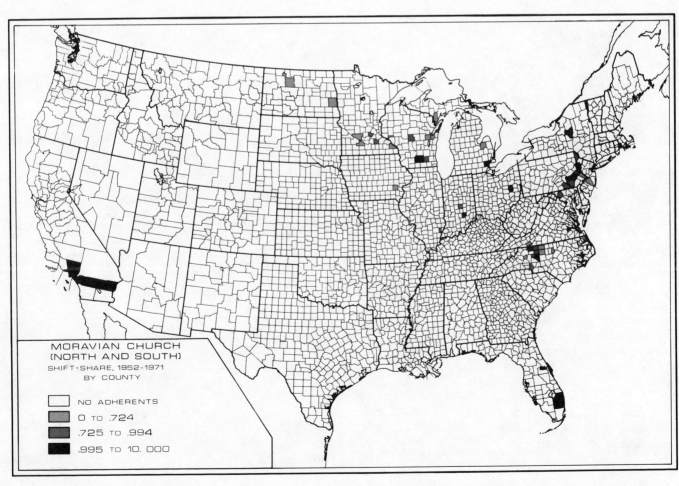

MORAVIAN CHURCH
(NORTH AND SOUTH)
SHIFT-SHARE, 1952-1971
BY COUNTY

NO ADHERENTS
0 TO .724
.725 TO .994
.995 TO 10. 000

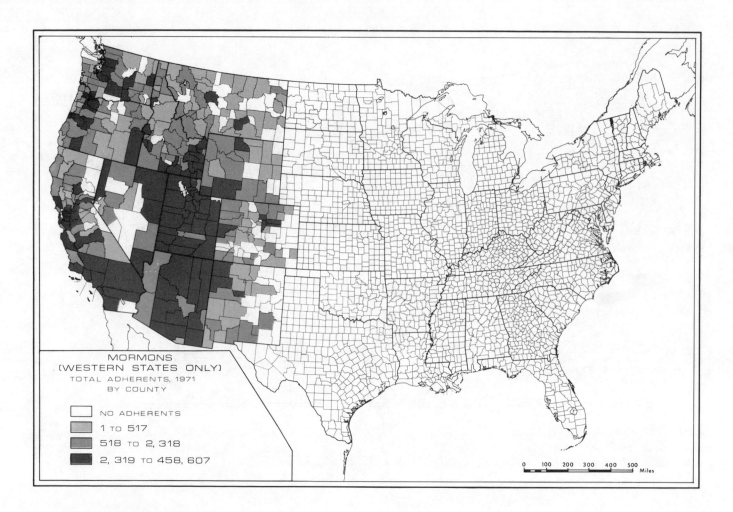

MORMONS
(WESTERN STATES ONLY)
TOTAL ADHERENTS, 1971
BY COUNTY

NO ADHERENTS
1 TO 517
518 TO 2,318
2,319 TO 458,607

0 100 200 300 400 500
Miles

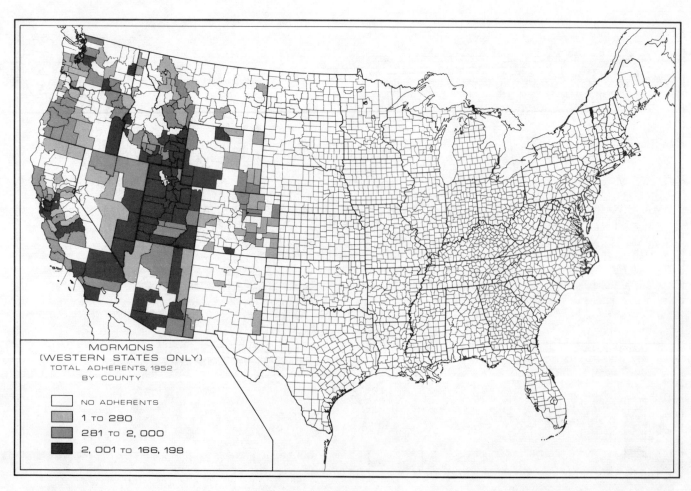

MORMONS
(WESTERN STATES ONLY)
TOTAL ADHERENTS, 1952
BY COUNTY

NO ADHERENTS
1 TO 280
281 TO 2,000
2,001 TO 166,198

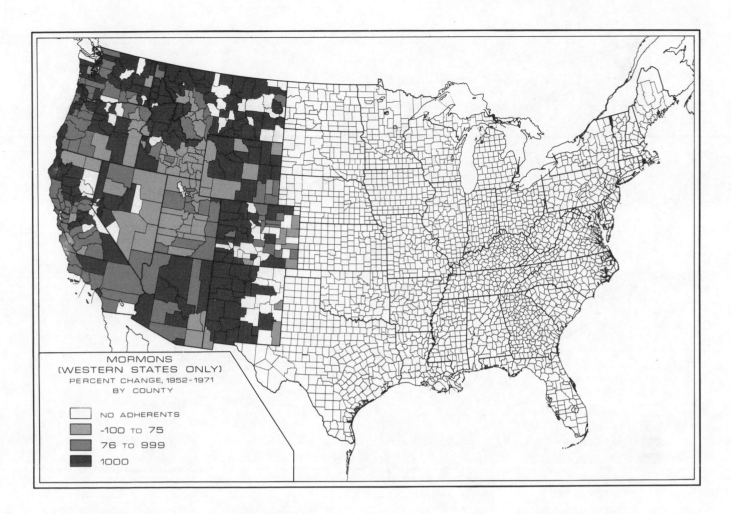

MORMONS
(WESTERN STATES ONLY)
PERCENT CHANGE, 1952-1971
BY COUNTY

NO ADHERENTS
-100 TO 75
76 TO 999
1000

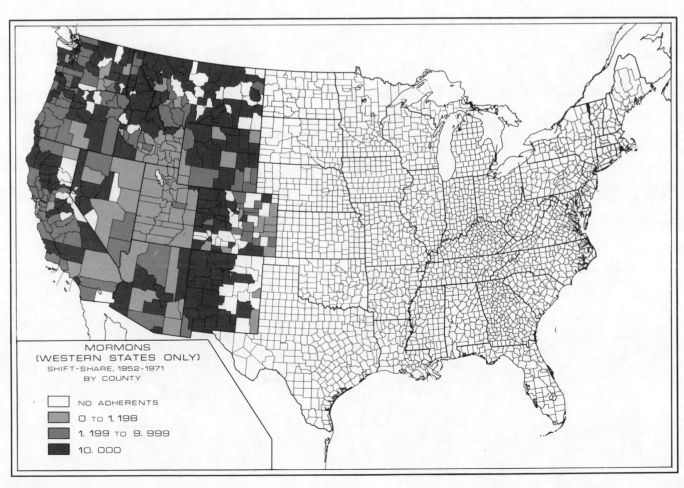

MORMONS
(WESTERN STATES ONLY)
SHIFT-SHARE, 1952-1971
BY COUNTY

NO ADHERENTS
0 TO 1.198
1.199 TO 9.999
10.000

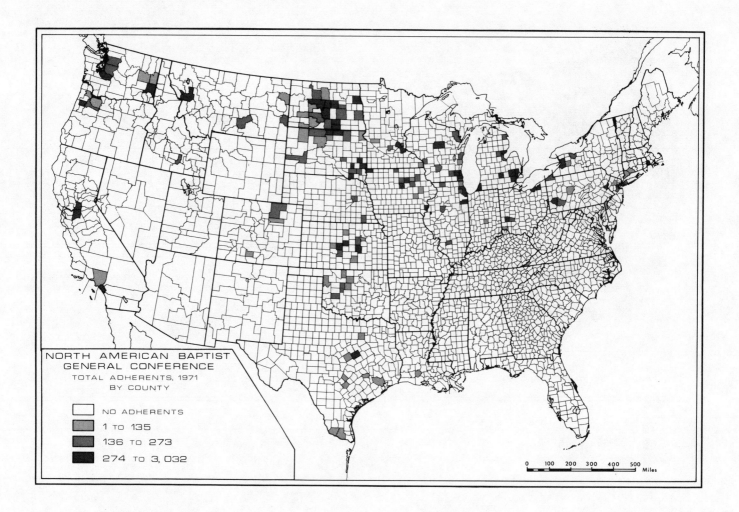

NORTH AMERICAN BAPTIST
GENERAL CONFERENCE
TOTAL ADHERENTS, 1971
BY COUNTY

NO ADHERENTS
1 TO 135
136 TO 273
274 TO 3,032

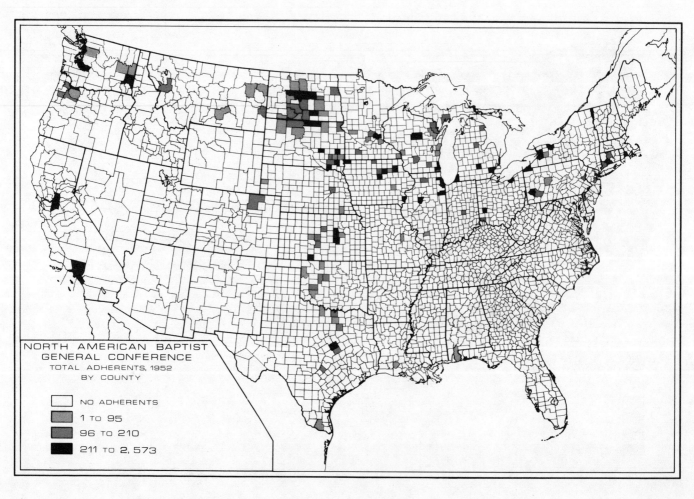

NORTH AMERICAN BAPTIST
GENERAL CONFERENCE
TOTAL ADHERENTS, 1952
BY COUNTY

NO ADHERENTS
1 TO 95
96 TO 210
211 TO 2,573

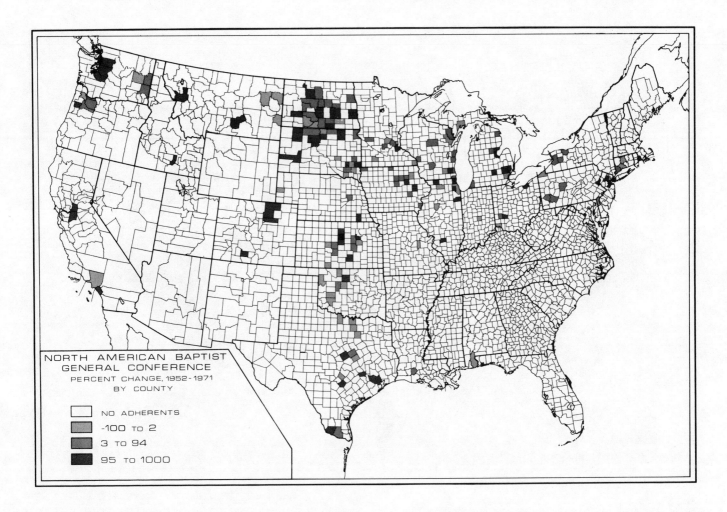

NORTH AMERICAN BAPTIST
GENERAL CONFERENCE
PERCENT CHANGE, 1952-1971
BY COUNTY

- NO ADHERENTS
- -100 TO 2
- 3 TO 94
- 95 TO 1000

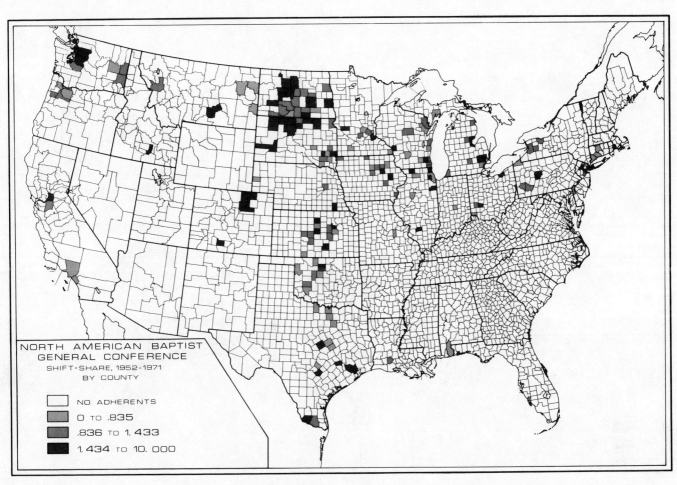

NORTH AMERICAN BAPTIST
GENERAL CONFERENCE
SHIFT-SHARE, 1952-1971
BY COUNTY

- NO ADHERENTS
- 0 TO .835
- .836 TO 1.433
- 1.434 TO 10.000

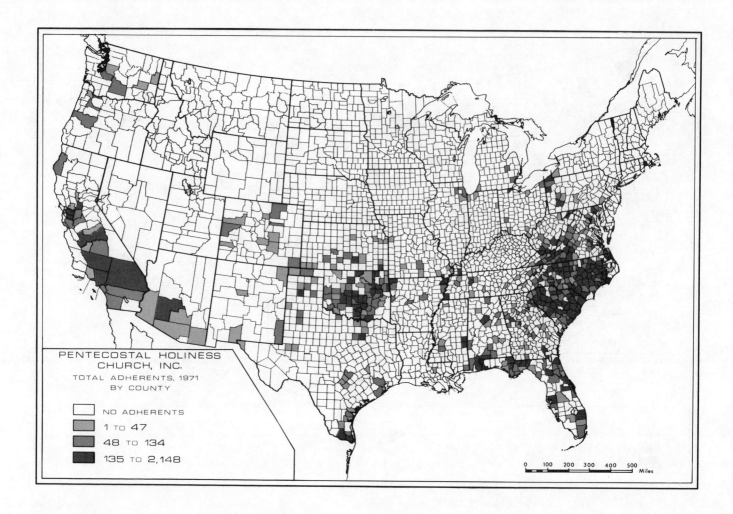

PENTECOSTAL HOLINESS
CHURCH, INC.

TOTAL ADHERENTS, 1971
BY COUNTY

NO ADHERENTS
1 TO 47
48 TO 134
135 TO 2,148

0 100 200 300 400 500
Miles

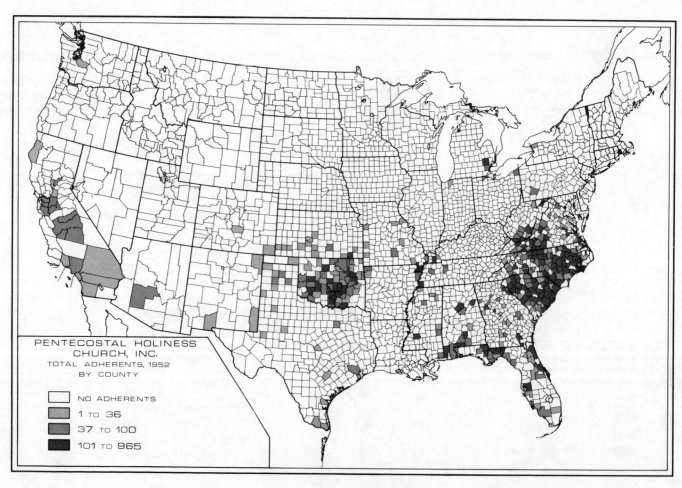

PENTECOSTAL HOLINESS
CHURCH, INC.

TOTAL ADHERENTS, 1952
BY COUNTY

NO ADHERENTS
1 TO 36
37 TO 100
101 TO 965

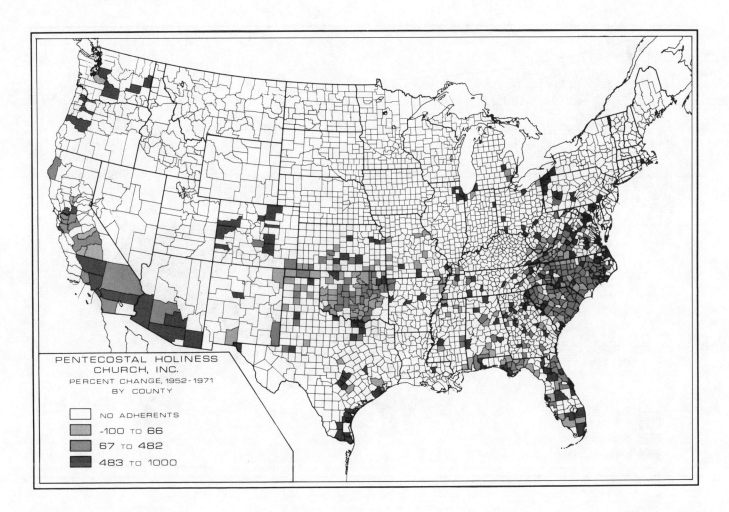

PENTECOSTAL HOLINESS
CHURCH, INC.

PERCENT CHANGE, 1952-1971
BY COUNTY

NO ADHERENTS
-100 TO 66
67 TO 482
483 TO 1000

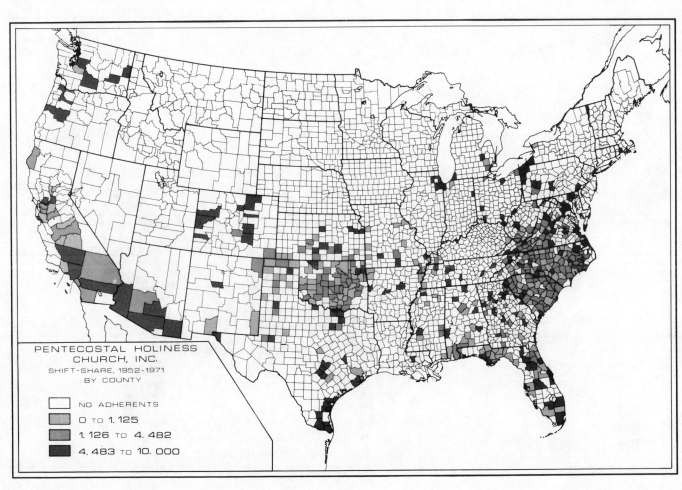

PENTECOSTAL HOLINESS
CHURCH, INC.

SHIFT-SHARE, 1952-1971
BY COUNTY

NO ADHERENTS
0 TO 1. 125
1. 126 TO 4. 482
4. 483 TO 10. 000

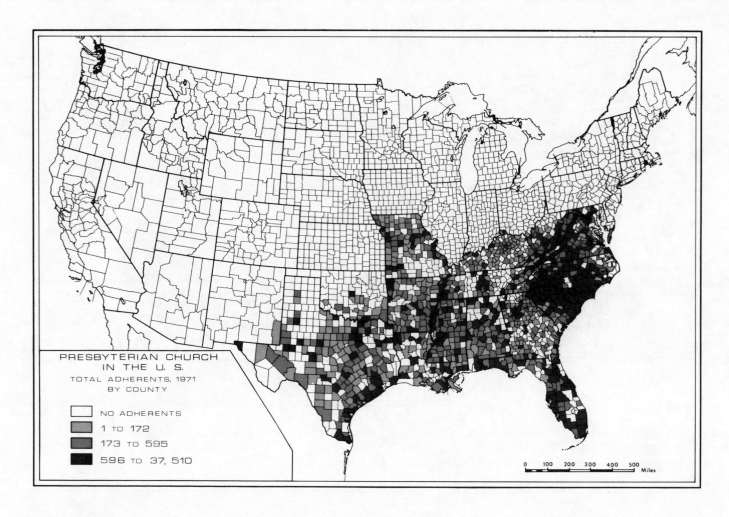

PRESBYTERIAN CHURCH
IN THE U. S.
TOTAL ADHERENTS, 1971
BY COUNTY

NO ADHERENTS
1 TO 172
173 TO 595
596 TO 37, 510

0   100   200   300   400   500
Miles

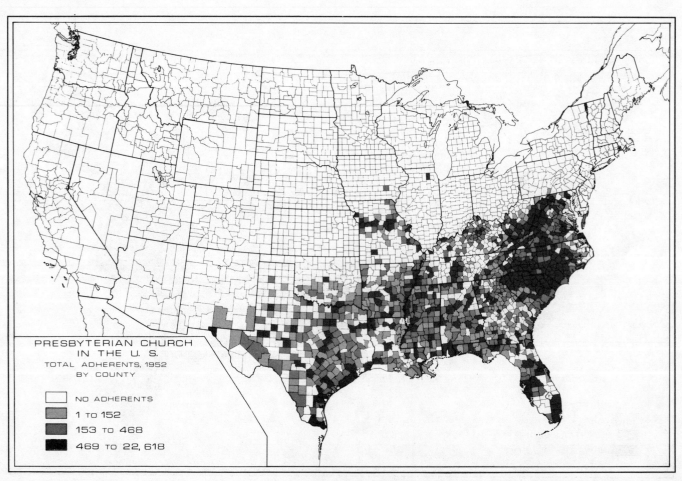

PRESBYTERIAN CHURCH
IN THE U. S.
TOTAL ADHERENTS, 1952
BY COUNTY

NO ADHERENTS
1 TO 152
153 TO 468
469 TO 22, 618

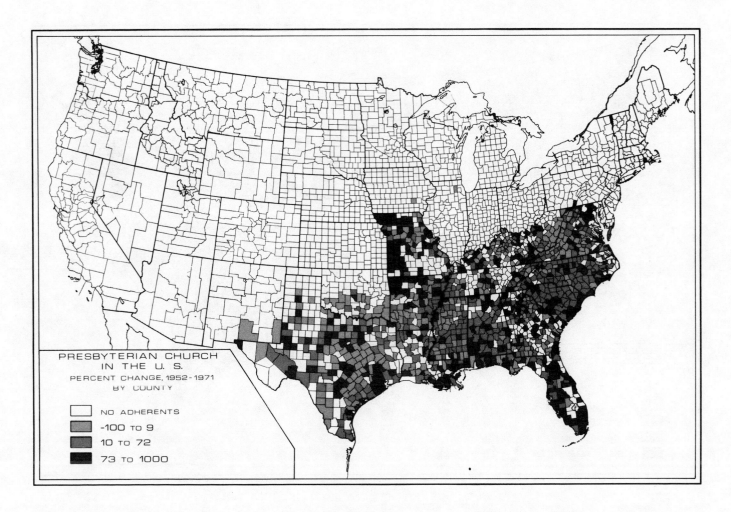

PRESBYTERIAN CHURCH
IN THE U. S.
PERCENT CHANGE, 1952-1971
BY COUNTY

NO ADHERENTS
-100 TO 9
10 TO 72
73 TO 1000

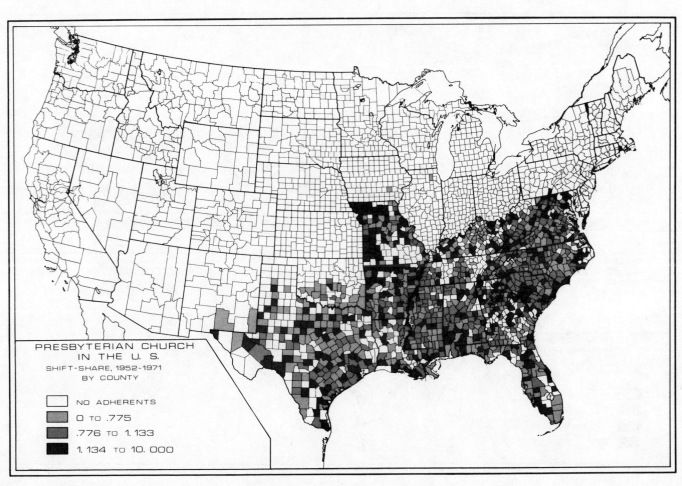

PRESBYTERIAN CHURCH
IN THE U. S.
SHIFT-SHARE, 1952-1971
BY COUNTY

NO ADHERENTS
0 TO .775
.776 TO 1.133
1.134 TO 10.000

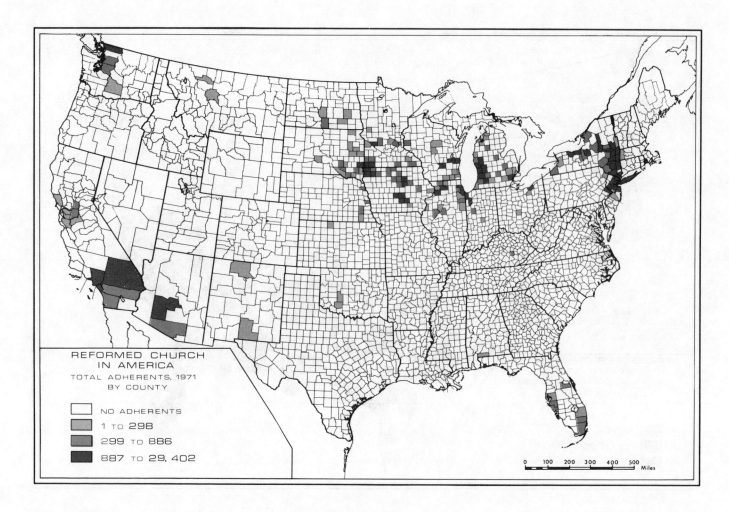

REFORMED CHURCH
IN AMERICA
TOTAL ADHERENTS, 1971
BY COUNTY

☐ NO ADHERENTS
1 TO 298
299 TO 886
887 TO 29, 402

0   100   200   300   400   500
Miles

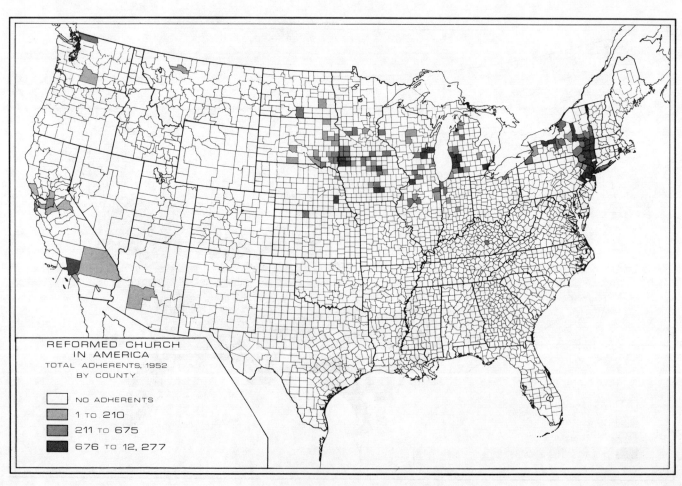

REFORMED CHURCH
IN AMERICA
TOTAL ADHERENTS, 1952
BY COUNTY

☐ NO ADHERENTS
1 TO 210
211 TO 675
676 TO 12, 277

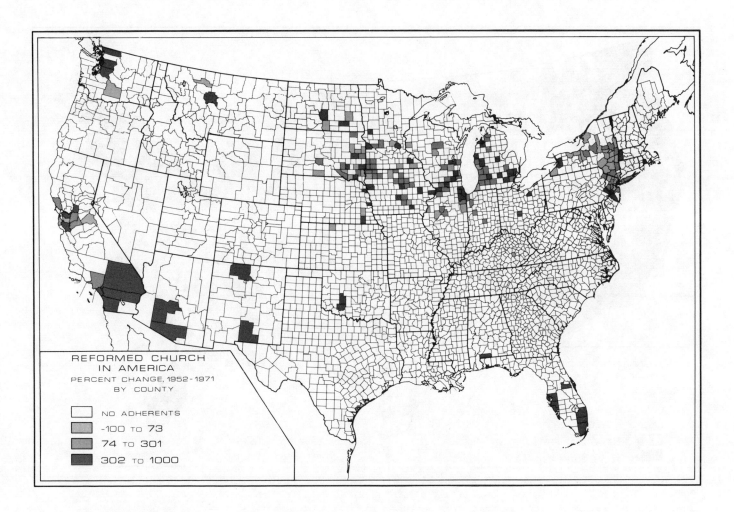

REFORMED CHURCH
IN AMERICA
PERCENT CHANGE, 1952-1971
BY COUNTY

NO ADHERENTS

-100 TO 73

74 TO 301

302 TO 1000

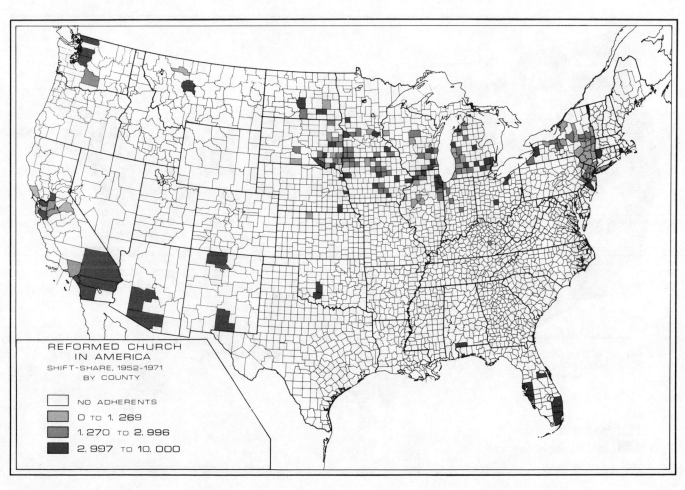

REFORMED CHURCH
IN AMERICA
SHIFT-SHARE, 1952-1971
BY COUNTY

NO ADHERENTS

0 TO 1. 269

1. 270 TO 2. 996

2. 997 TO 10. 000

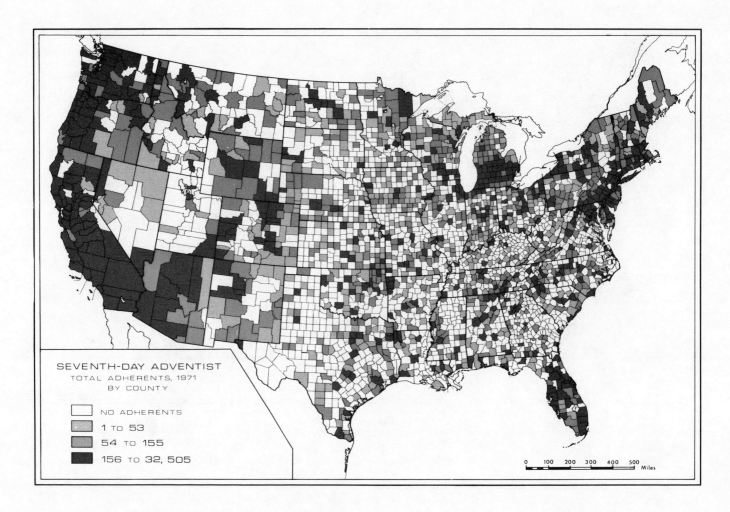

SEVENTH-DAY ADVENTIST
TOTAL ADHERENTS, 1971
BY COUNTY

NO ADHERENTS
1 TO 53
54 TO 155
156 TO 32,505

0 100 200 300 400 500
Miles

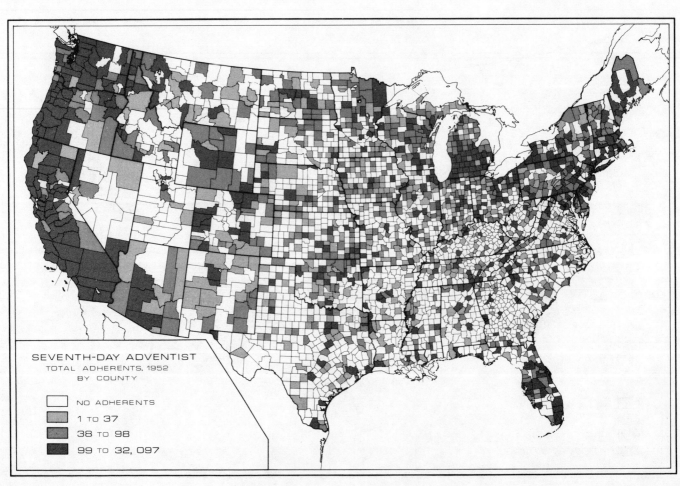

SEVENTH-DAY ADVENTIST
TOTAL ADHERENTS, 1952
BY COUNTY

NO ADHERENTS
1 TO 37
38 TO 98
99 TO 32,097

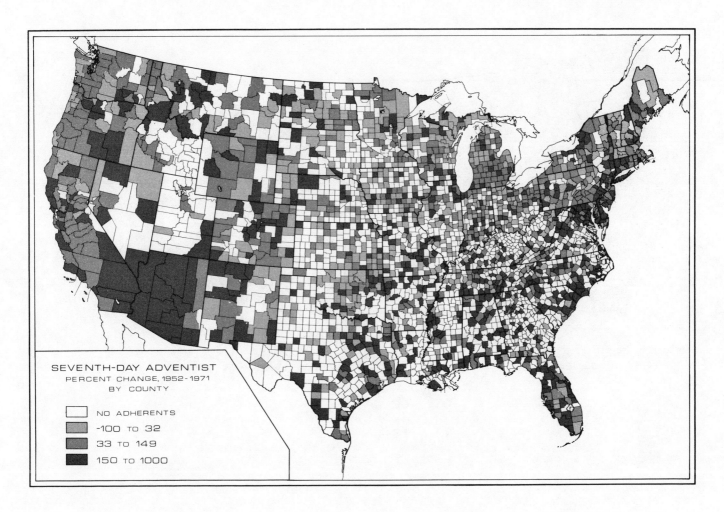

SEVENTH-DAY ADVENTIST
PERCENT CHANGE, 1952-1971
BY COUNTY

- NO ADHERENTS
- -100 TO 32
- 33 TO 149
- 150 TO 1000

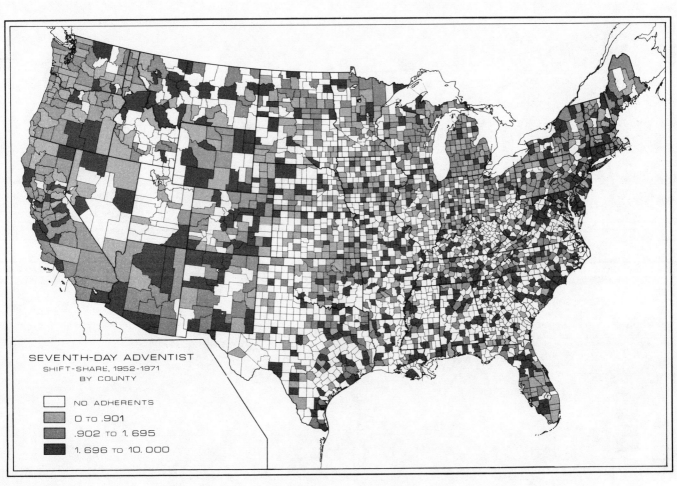

SEVENTH-DAY ADVENTIST
SHIFT-SHARE, 1952-1971
BY COUNTY

- NO ADHERENTS
- 0 TO .901
- .902 TO 1.695
- 1.696 TO 10.000

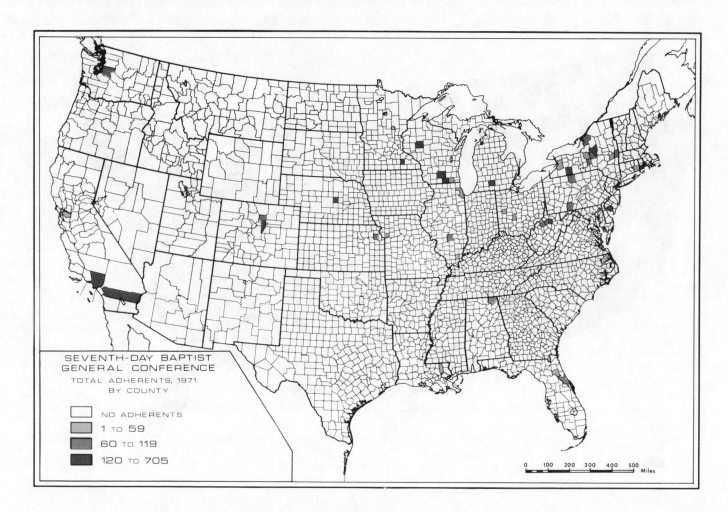

SEVENTH-DAY BAPTIST
GENERAL CONFERENCE

TOTAL ADHERENTS, 1971
BY COUNTY

NO ADHERENTS
1 TO 59
60 TO 119
120 TO 705

0   100   200   300   400   500
Miles

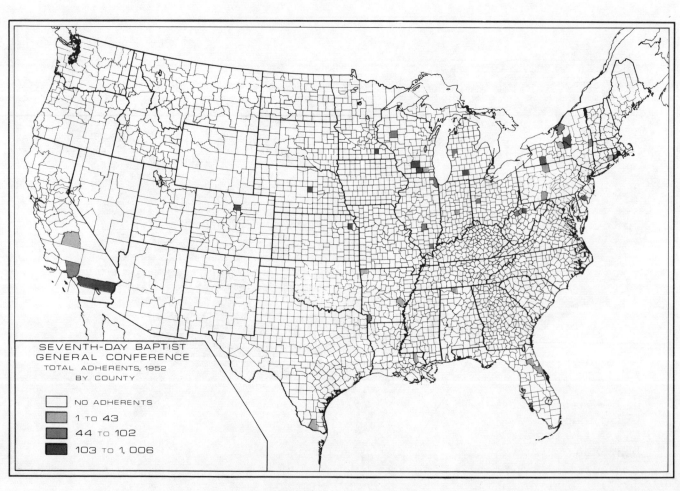

SEVENTH-DAY BAPTIST
GENERAL CONFERENCE

TOTAL ADHERENTS, 1952
BY COUNTY

NO ADHERENTS
1 TO 43
44 TO 102
103 TO 1,006

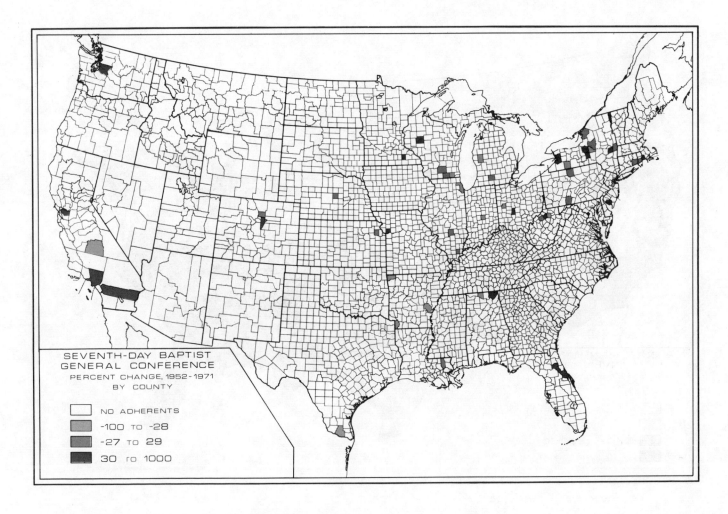

SEVENTH-DAY BAPTIST
GENERAL CONFERENCE
PERCENT CHANGE, 1952-1971
BY COUNTY

NO ADHERENTS
-100 TO -28
-27 TO 29
30 TO 1000

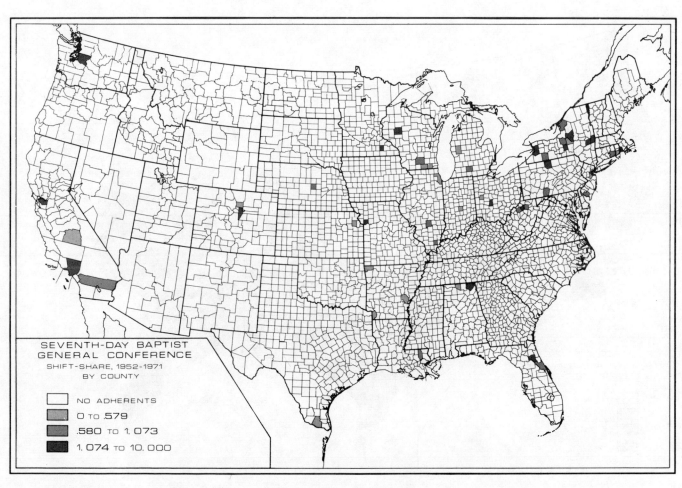

SEVENTH-DAY BAPTIST
GENERAL CONFERENCE
SHIFT-SHARE, 1952-1971
BY COUNTY

NO ADHERENTS
0 TO .579
.580 TO 1.073
1.074 TO 10.000

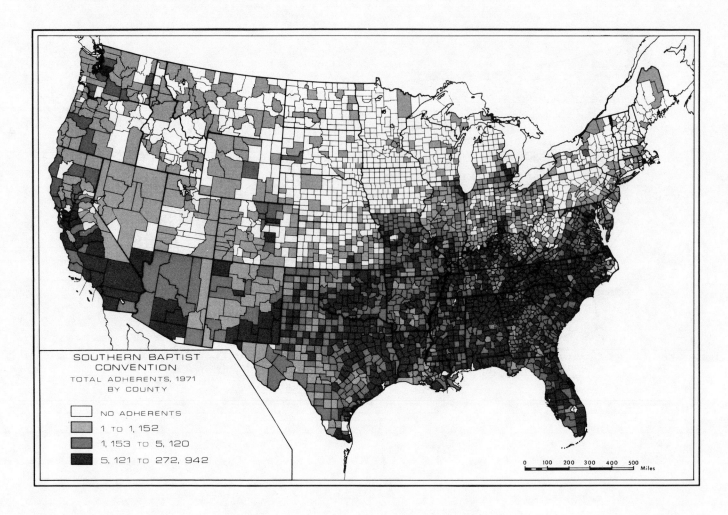

SOUTHERN BAPTIST
CONVENTION
TOTAL ADHERENTS, 1971
BY COUNTY

NO ADHERENTS
1 TO 1,152
1,153 TO 5,120
5,121 TO 272,942

0 100 200 300 400 500
Miles

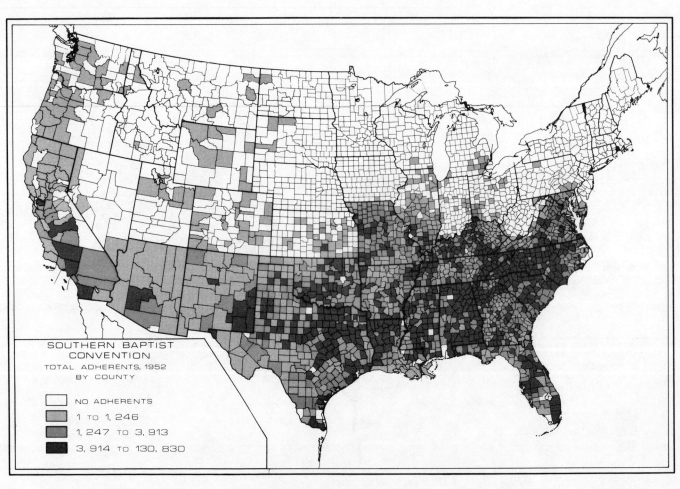

SOUTHERN BAPTIST
CONVENTION
TOTAL ADHERENTS, 1952
BY COUNTY

NO ADHERENTS
1 TO 1,246
1,247 TO 3,913
3,914 TO 130,830

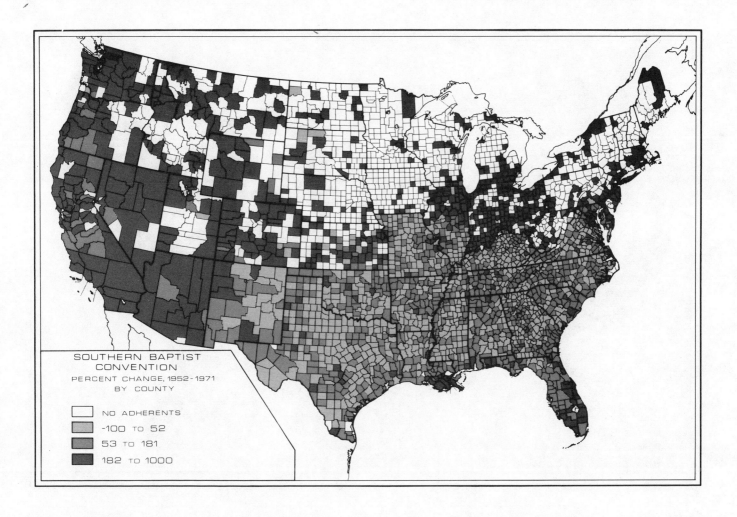

SOUTHERN BAPTIST
CONVENTION

PERCENT CHANGE, 1952-1971
BY COUNTY

NO ADHERENTS
-100 TO 52
53 TO 181
182 TO 1000

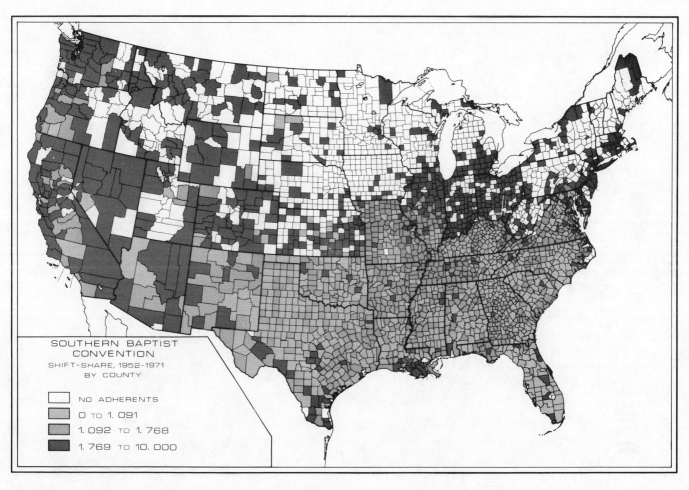

SOUTHERN BAPTIST
CONVENTION

SHIFT-SHARE, 1952-1971
BY COUNTY

NO ADHERENTS
0 TO 1.091
1.092 TO 1.768
1.769 TO 10.000

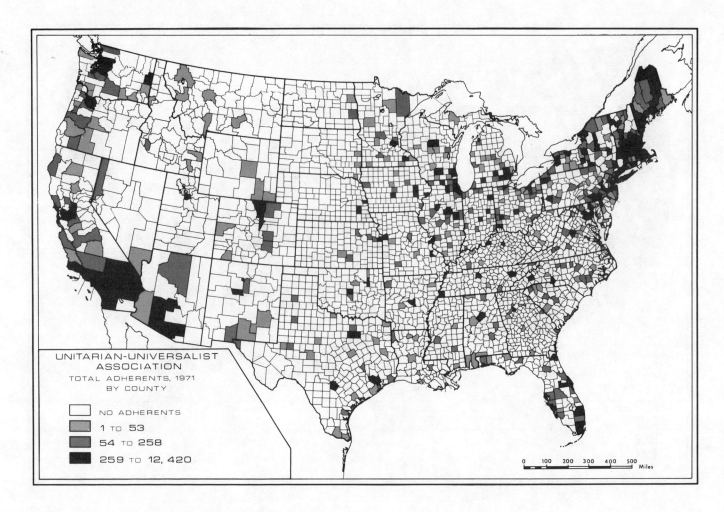

UNITARIAN-UNIVERSALIST
ASSOCIATION
TOTAL ADHERENTS, 1971
BY COUNTY

- NO ADHERENTS
- 1 TO 53
- 54 TO 258
- 259 TO 12,420

0 100 200 300 400 500 Miles

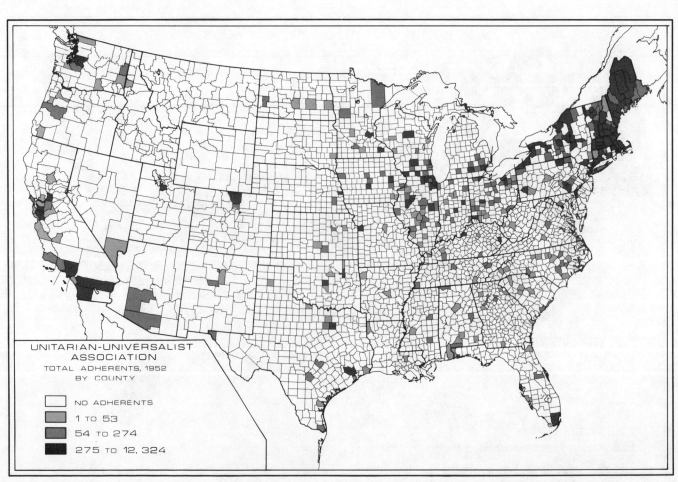

UNITARIAN-UNIVERSALIST
ASSOCIATION
TOTAL ADHERENTS, 1952
BY COUNTY

- NO ADHERENTS
- 1 TO 53
- 54 TO 274
- 275 TO 12,324

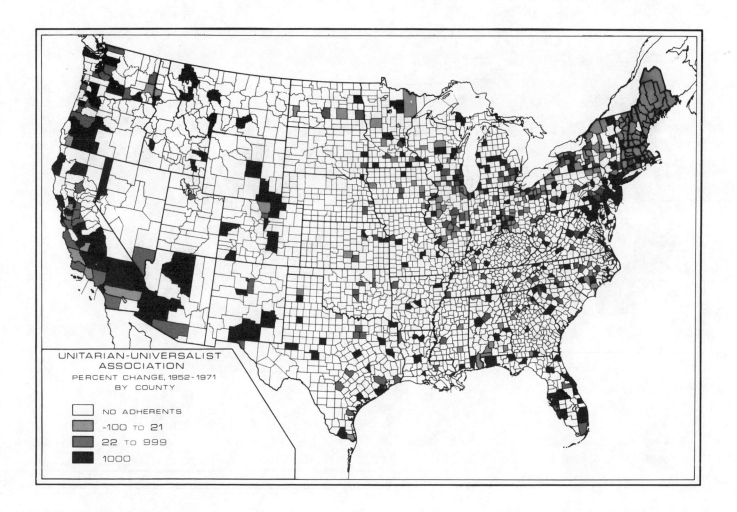

UNITARIAN-UNIVERSALIST
ASSOCIATION
PERCENT CHANGE, 1952-1971
BY COUNTY

NO ADHERENTS
-100 TO 21
22 TO 999
1000

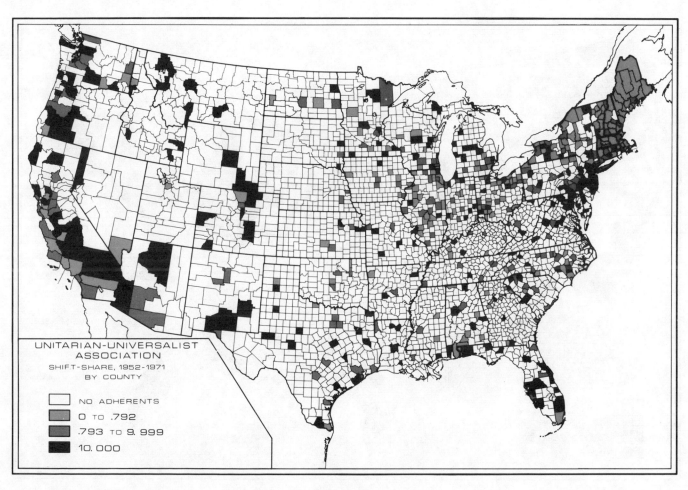

UNITARIAN-UNIVERSALIST
ASSOCIATION
SHIFT-SHARE, 1952-1971
BY COUNTY

NO ADHERENTS
0 TO .792
.793 TO 9.999
10.000

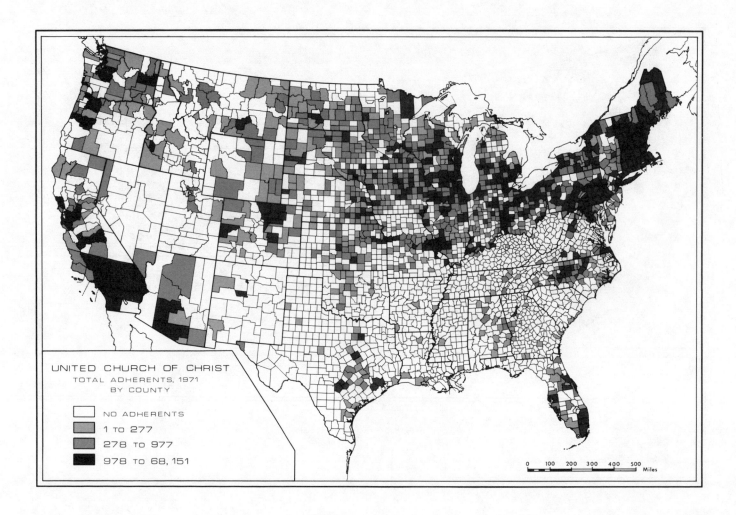

UNITED CHURCH OF CHRIST
TOTAL ADHERENTS, 1971
BY COUNTY

NO ADHERENTS
1 TO 277
278 TO 977
978 TO 68,151

0   100   200   300   400   500   Miles

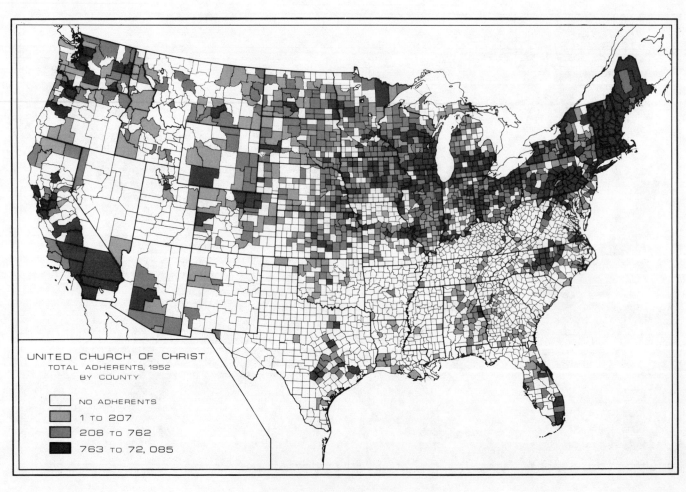

UNITED CHURCH OF CHRIST
TOTAL ADHERENTS, 1952
BY COUNTY

NO ADHERENTS
1 TO 207
208 TO 762
763 TO 72,085

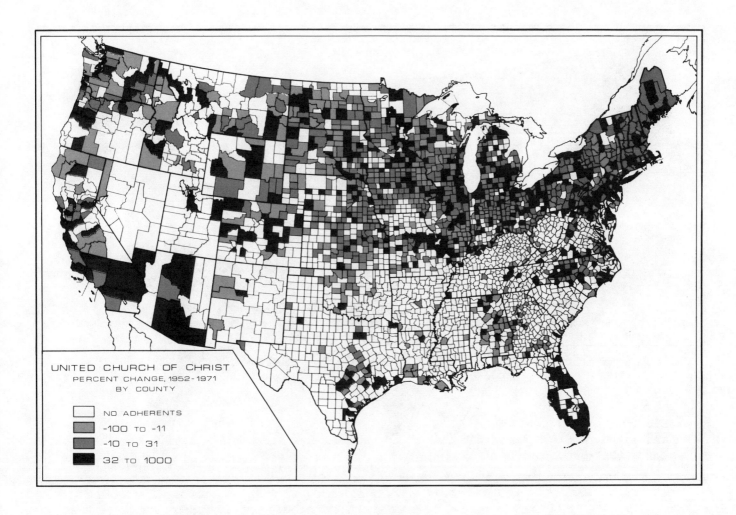

UNITED CHURCH OF CHRIST
PERCENT CHANGE, 1952-1971
BY COUNTY

NO ADHERENTS
-100 TO -11
-10 TO 31
32 TO 1000

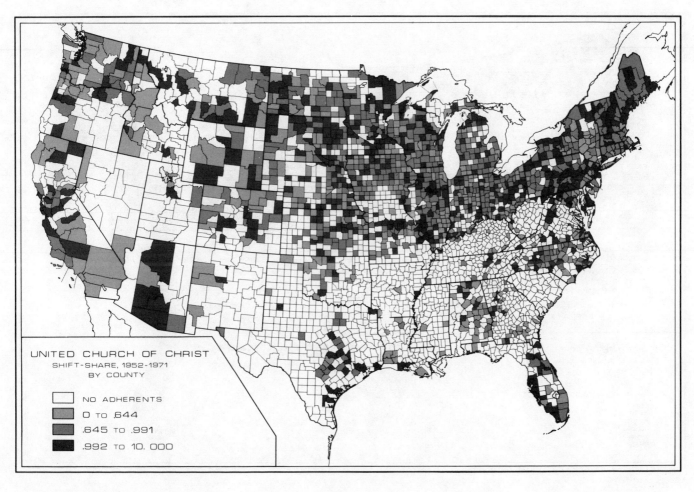

UNITED CHURCH OF CHRIST
SHIFT-SHARE, 1952-1971
BY COUNTY

NO ADHERENTS
0 TO .644
.645 TO .991
.992 TO 10.000

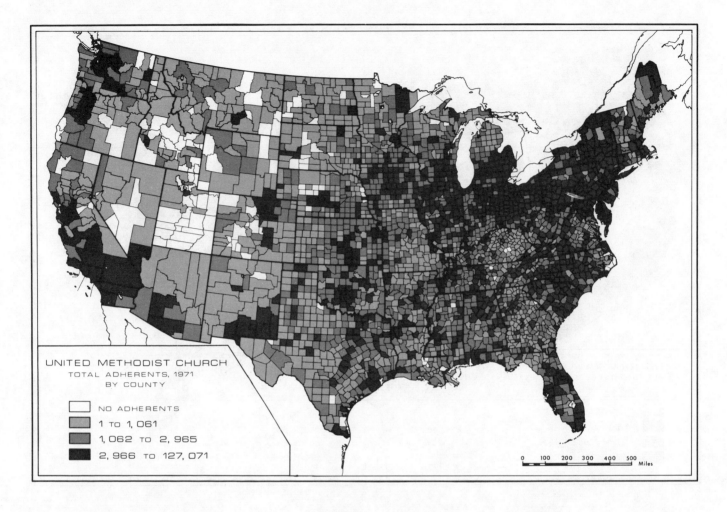

UNITED METHODIST CHURCH
TOTAL ADHERENTS, 1971
BY COUNTY

NO ADHERENTS
1 TO 1,061
1,062 TO 2,965
2,966 TO 127,071

0 100 200 300 400 500 Miles

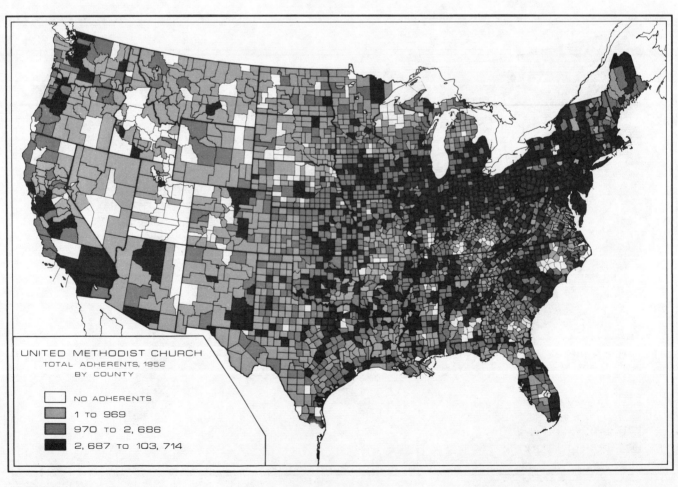

UNITED METHODIST CHURCH
TOTAL ADHERENTS, 1952
BY COUNTY

NO ADHERENTS
1 TO 969
970 TO 2,686
2,687 TO 103,714

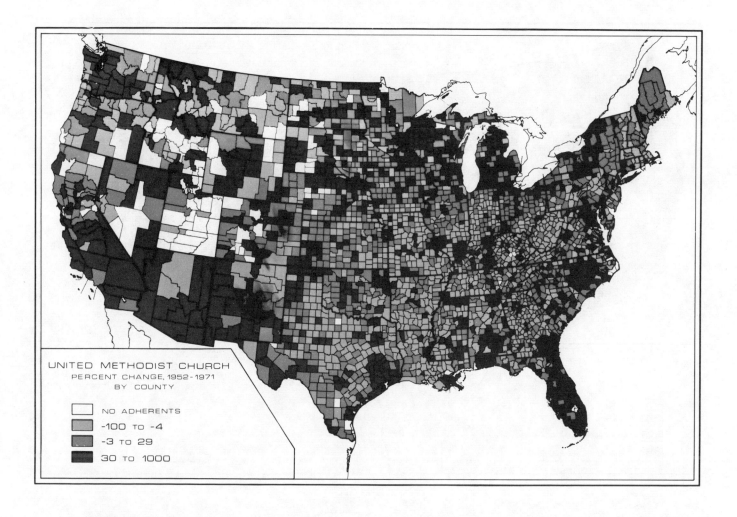

UNITED METHODIST CHURCH
PERCENT CHANGE, 1952-1971
BY COUNTY

NO ADHERENTS
-100 TO -4
-3 TO 29
30 TO 1000

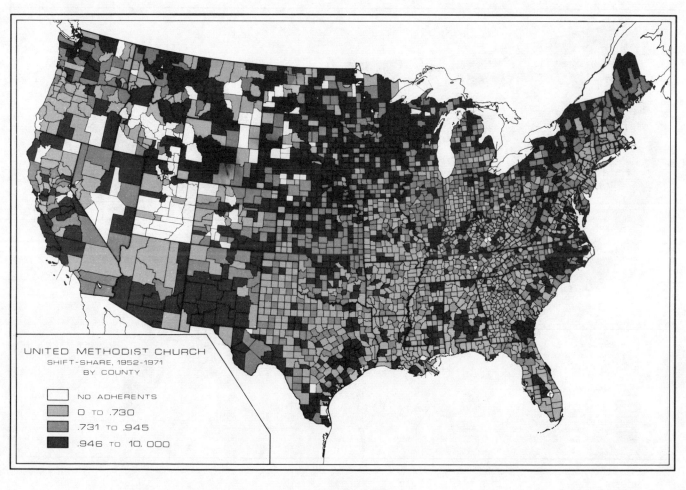

UNITED METHODIST CHURCH
SHIFT-SHARE, 1952-1971
BY COUNTY

NO ADHERENTS
0 TO .730
.731 TO .945
.946 TO 10.000

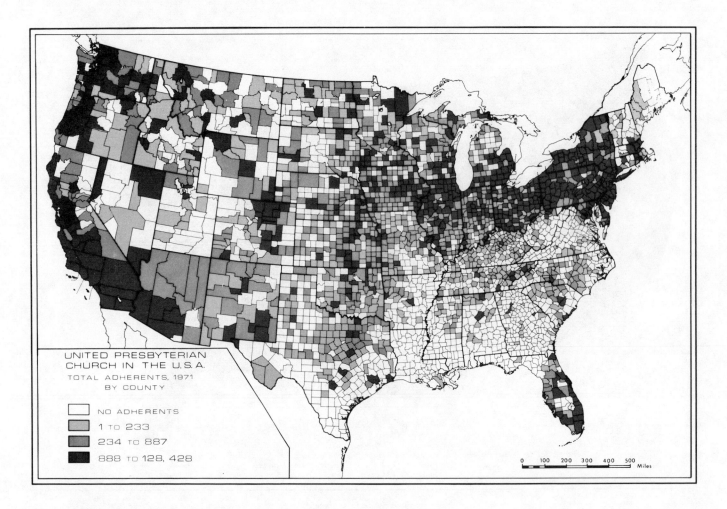

UNITED PRESBYTERIAN
CHURCH IN THE U.S.A.
TOTAL ADHERENTS, 1971
BY COUNTY

NO ADHERENTS
1 TO 233
234 TO 887
888 TO 128, 428

0 100 200 300 400 500
Miles

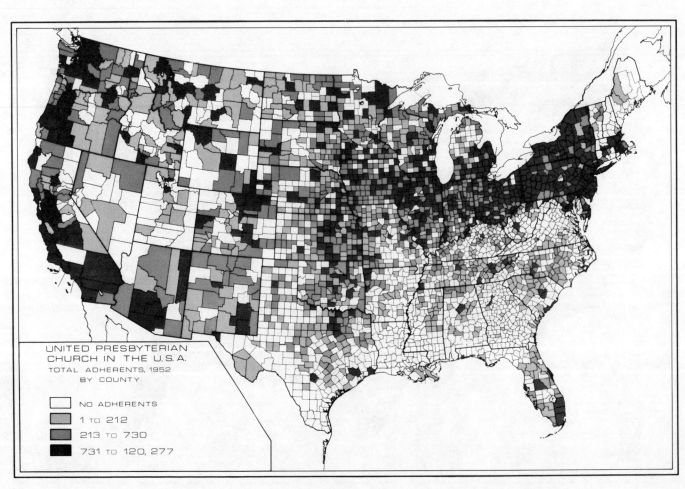

UNITED PRESBYTERIAN
CHURCH IN THE U.S.A.
TOTAL ADHERENTS, 1952
BY COUNTY

NO ADHERENTS
1 TO 212
213 TO 730
731 TO 120, 277

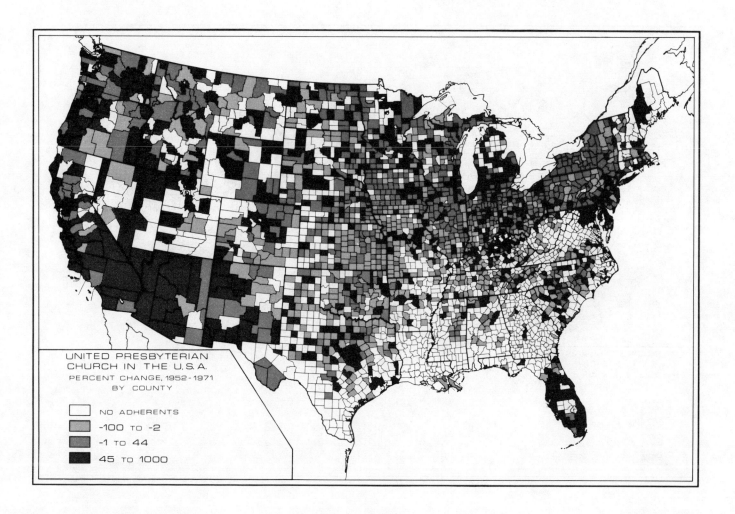

UNITED PRESBYTERIAN
CHURCH IN THE U.S.A.
PERCENT CHANGE, 1952-1971
BY COUNTY

☐ NO ADHERENTS
▨ -100 TO -2
▨ -1 TO 44
■ 45 TO 1000

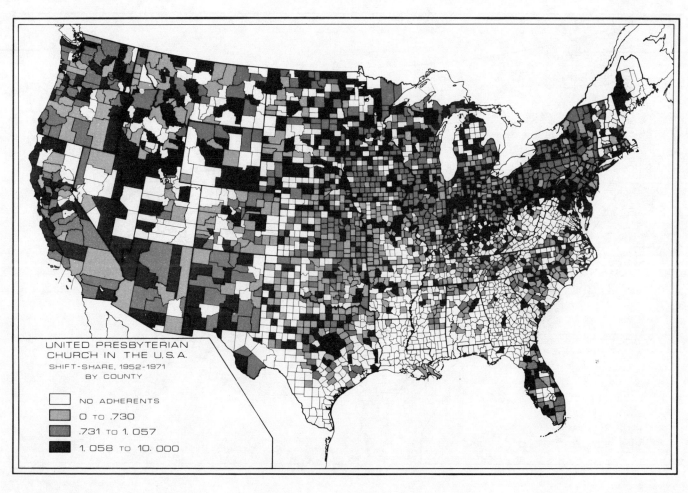

UNITED PRESBYTERIAN
CHURCH IN THE U.S.A.
SHIFT-SHARE, 1952-1971
BY COUNTY

☐ NO ADHERENTS
▨ 0 TO .730
▨ .731 TO 1.057
■ 1.058 TO 10.000

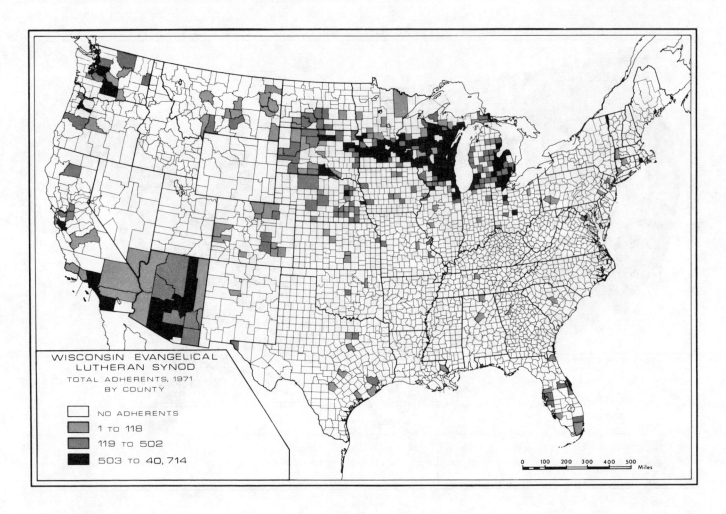

WISCONSIN EVANGELICAL
LUTHERAN SYNOD
TOTAL ADHERENTS, 1971
BY COUNTY

NO ADHERENTS
1 TO 118
119 TO 502
503 TO 40,714

0   100 200 300 400 500
Miles

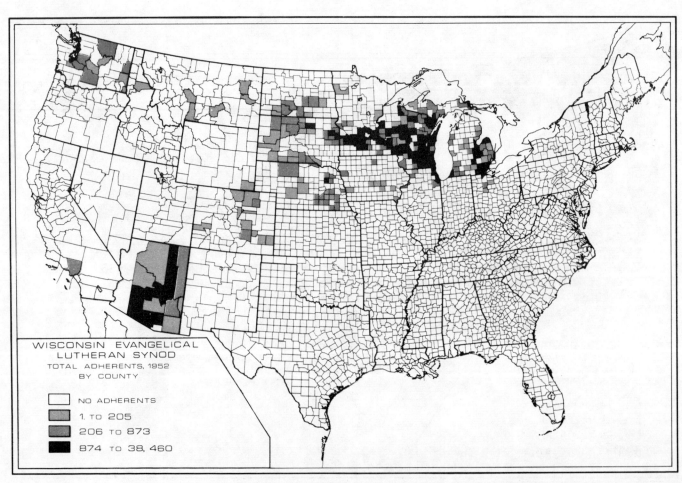

WISCONSIN EVANGELICAL
LUTHERAN SYNOD
TOTAL ADHERENTS, 1952
BY COUNTY

NO ADHERENTS
1. TO 205
206 TO 873
874 TO 38,460

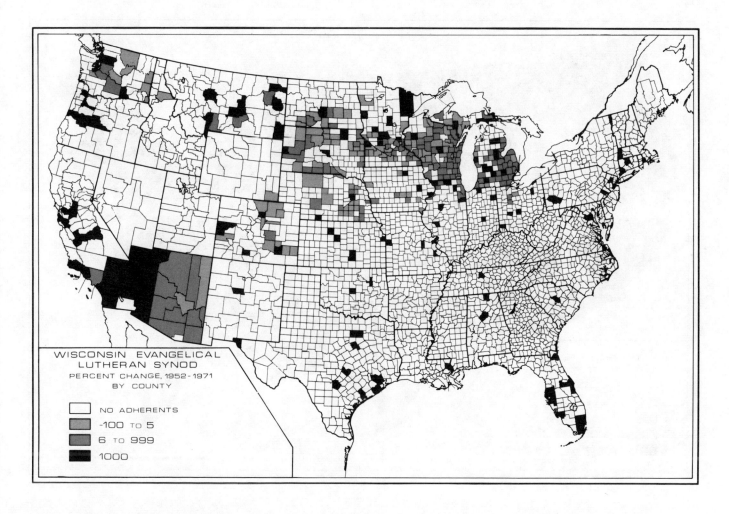

WISCONSIN EVANGELICAL
LUTHERAN SYNOD
PERCENT CHANGE, 1952-1971
BY COUNTY

	NO ADHERENTS
	-100 TO 5
	6 TO 999
	1000

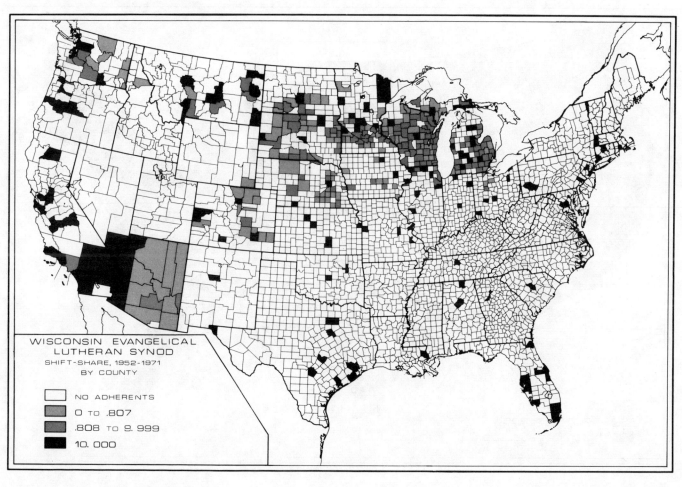

WISCONSIN EVANGELICAL
LUTHERAN SYNOD
SHIFT-SHARE, 1952-1971
BY COUNTY

	NO ADHERENTS
	0 TO .807
	.808 TO 9.999
	10.000

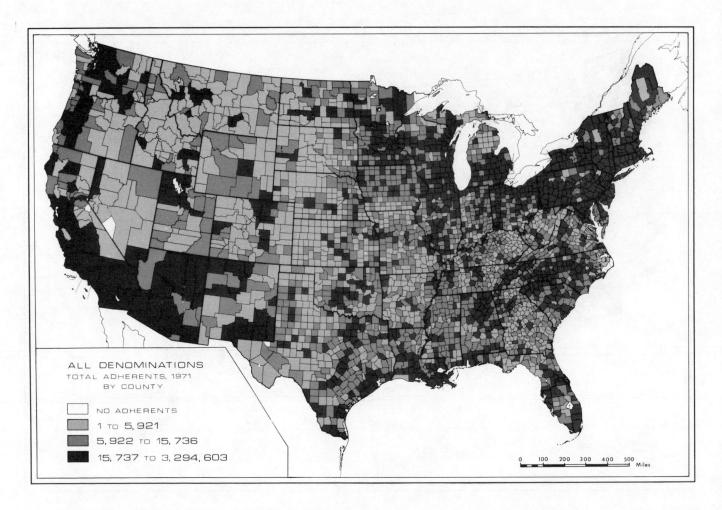

ALL DENOMINATIONS
TOTAL ADHERENTS, 1971
BY COUNTY

NO ADHERENTS
1 TO 5,921
5,922 TO 15,736
15,737 TO 3,294,603

0 100 200 300 400 500
Miles

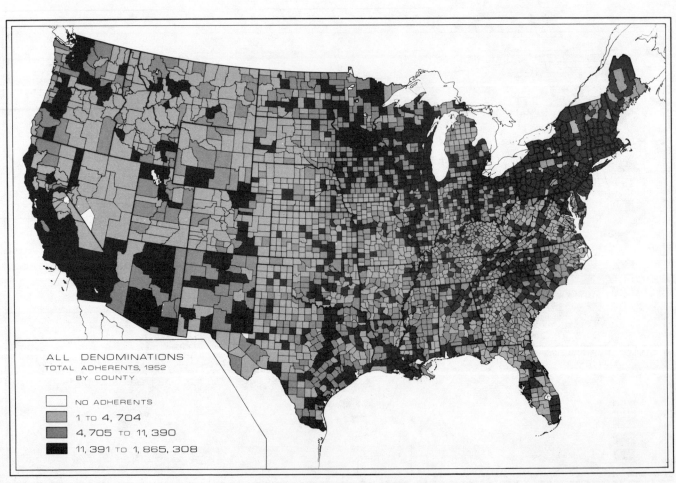

ALL DENOMINATIONS
TOTAL ADHERENTS, 1952
BY COUNTY

NO ADHERENTS
1 TO 4,704
4,705 TO 11,390
11,391 TO 1,865,308

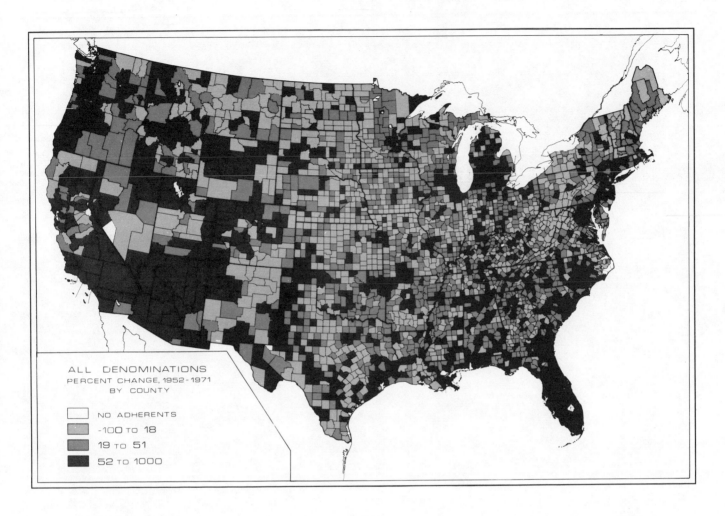

ALL DENOMINATIONS
PERCENT CHANGE, 1952-1971
BY COUNTY

NO ADHERENTS
-100 TO 18
19 TO 51
52 TO 1000

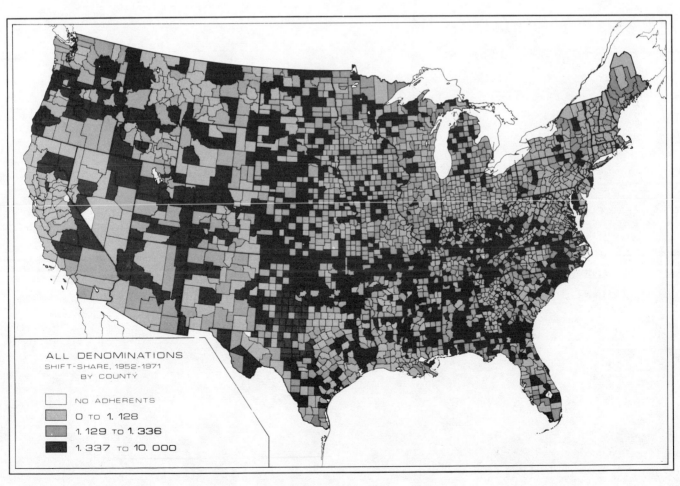

ALL DENOMINATIONS
SHIFT-SHARE, 1952-1971
BY COUNTY

NO ADHERENTS
0 TO 1. 128
1. 129 TO 1. 336
1. 337 TO 10. 000